THE BEST OF

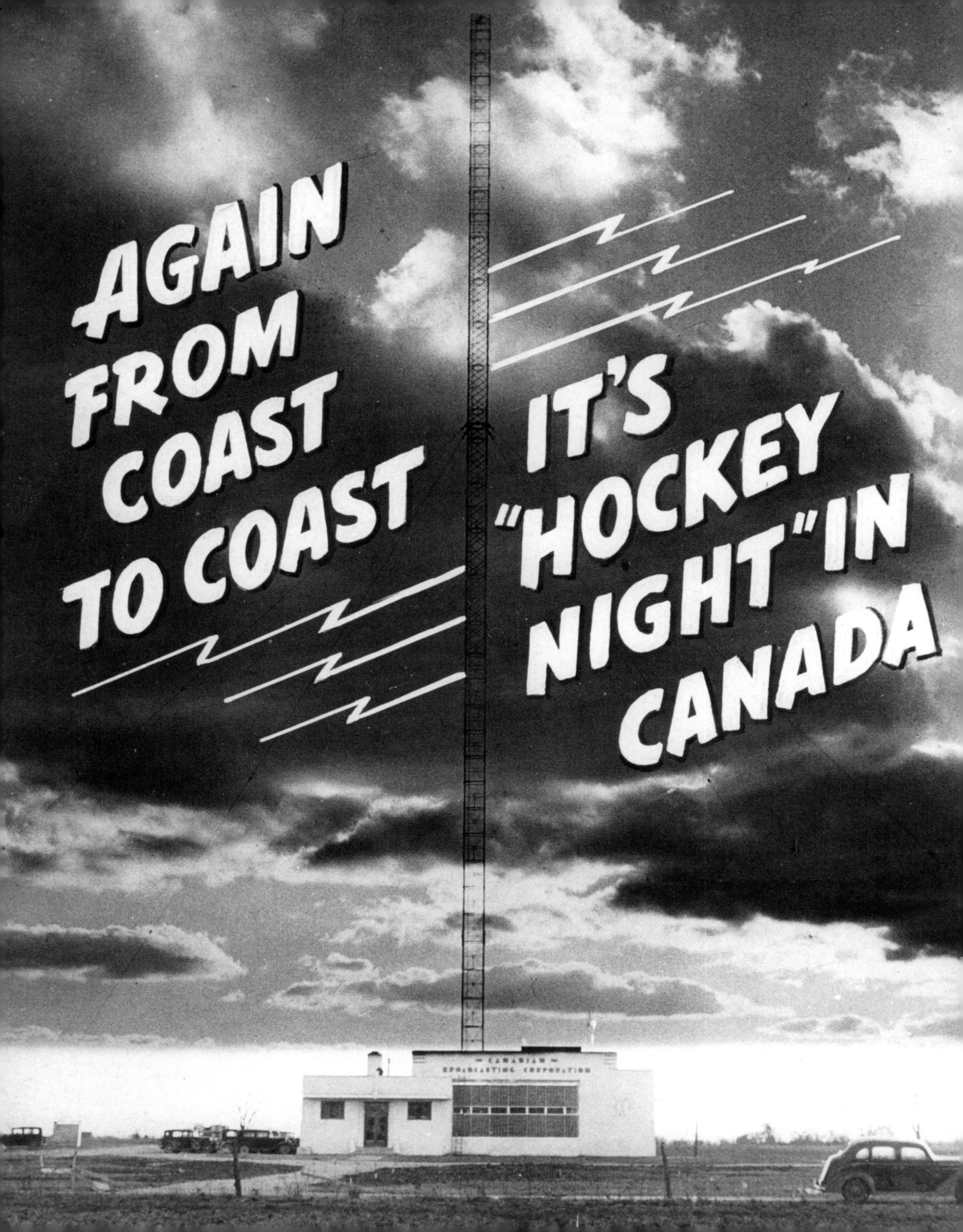
AGAIN FROM COAST TO COAST
IT'S "HOCKEY NIGHT" IN CANADA
CANADIAN BROADCASTING CORPORATION

THE BEST OF
HOCKEY NIGHT
IN CANADA

STEPHEN COLE

CBCtelevision

McArthur & Company

TORONTO

First published in Canada in 2003 by
McArthur & Company
322 King Street West, Suite 402
Toronto, Ontario
M5V 1J2
www.mcarthur-co.com

National Library of Canada Cataloguing in Publication

Cole, Stephen
        The best of Hockey night in Canada / written by Stephen Cole.

Includes index.
ISBN 1-55278-408-8

        1. Hockey night in Canada (Television program)--History. 2. Hockey night
in Canada (Radio program)--History. 3. Sportscasters--Canada--History.
4. Television broadcasting of sports--Canada--History. 5. Radio broadcasting of sports--Canada--History. I. Title.

GV742.3.C64 2003   070.4'49796962'0971   C2003-905969-3

Photography Editor and Story Consultant: Paul Patskou
Interior Design and Composition: Tania Craan
Printed in Canada by Friesens

The publisher would like to acknowledge the financial support of the Government of Canada through the Book Publishing Industry
Development Program, the Canada Council, and the Ontario Arts Council for our publishing activities. We also acknowledge the
Government of Ontario through the Ontario Media Development Corporation Ontario Book Initiative.

10 9 8 7 6 5 4 3 2 1

In memory of Danny Gallivan and Foster and Bill Hewitt

ACKNOWLEDGMENTS

This book would not have been possible without the "yeoman service," as Danny Gallivan would say, of photography and story editor Paul Patskou. Paul not only chased down every one of the photographs and televised images in this book, but he also helped select the stories and provided the author with generous access to his vast archives of *Hockey Night in Canada* games, Molson Archives, and *Leaf's TV* archives. In addition, Paul was of great help in "overtime," assisting with the editing and photo captions. Thank you, Paul!

My primary source for *The Best of Hockey Night in Canada* was HNIC itself. Because of my own life-long interest in the program and grateful access to Paul Patskou's HNIC collection, I was able to listen to or re-watch more than 60 of the games highlighted here, including some of those that I saw as a child or teenager, or reported on recently. Many of the quotes in this book are transcribed from tapes of radio or television broadcasts, or from interviews with various players and coaches either done myself or as seen on HNIC.

No one would want to attempt an anecdotal chronicle of *Hockey Night in Canada* without reading Scott Young's valuable resource, *The Boys of Saturday Night*. In addition, I made use of Trent Frayne's *The Mad Men of Hockey*, Jack Batten's *Hockey Dynasty*, Chrys Goyens and Allan Turowetz's *Lions in Winter*, John Robert Columbo's *Columbo's Book of Canadian Quotations*, Dick Beddoes' *Hockey's Greatest Stories*, Dick Irvin's *Now Back to You Dick*, Lawrence Martin's *Mario*, and Peter Gzowski's *The Game of Our Lives*.

Along with game tapes and books, newspaper articles of the time were enormously helpful. In addition to the stories I've written for *TV Guide*, the *National Post* and the *Globe and Mail*, I also made use of articles from the *Globe and Mail*, the *Toronto Star*, *Weekend Magazine*, *Canadian Magazine*, the *Montreal Gazette*, *Hockey News*, *Maclean's*, *Hockey Digest*, the *New York Post*, the *Winnipeg Free Press*, the *Boston Globe*, and the *National Post*.

Global TV's documentary and Radio Canada's docudrama on the Rocket Richard story were excellent sources, as were several segments of the *Hot Stove League* (in French and English), courtesy of Paul Patskou. NESN-TV, the Boston superstation, had a wonderful account of the Bruins-Canadiens playoff, and the CBC production, *Sports Journal: History of Hockey Night in Canada* was a great resource for writing about the many Canadian players on the Detroit Red Wings team in the early days. Parts of this book were first published in my own books, *Slapshots* (Penguin, 1993), *The Last Hurrah: A Celebration of Hockey's Greatest Season—1966–67* (Penguin, 1995) and *Here's Looking at Us: Celebrating 50 Years of CBC TV* (McClelland & Stewart, 2002). I've also contributed to *Maple Leaf Gardens: Memories & Dreams* (Dan Diamond and Associates, 1999) and *Total Hockey* (Total Sports, 2000).

Grateful thanks to Kim McArthur and the entire enthusiastic team at McArthur & Company, my agent Dean Cooke, and also to Tania Craan, who designed this book, and Pamela Erlichman, who edited it.

Finally, an enormous thank you to Ron MacLean, Don Cherry, Harry Neale and Bob Cole, who had me in one night to watch them at work on HNIC, as well as to Kelly Hrudey, Dick Irvin, Jr., Brian McFarlane, Gérald Renaud, Frank Selke, Jr., Harry Neale and Bob Cole, who contributed their reminiscences to this book. David Hainline and Barbara Brown of CBC Merchandising were hugely helpful in tracking down many of the CBC photos, as well as "A Day in the Life of HNIC," the Ken Danby painting and article, and the classic "Happy Motoring Song." Many thanks to producers past and present, and to the entire staff of *Hockey Night in Canada* for their advice and support.

TABLE OF CONTENTS

Television
1960–61 to 1969–70

Television
1990–91 to Present 121

RADIO
1931–32 to 1951–52

THE IMPERIAL DEALER

VOLUME 5, NO.8

NOVEMBER, 1938

IMPERIAL DEALER

HOCKEY NIGHT IN CANADA
SEE PAGE 3

FOSTERING A TRADITION

November 12, 1931

In 1923 Foster Hewitt returned to the *Toronto Daily Star* after a gruelling day's work and was nabbed for an assignment no one else wanted: hurry to Mutual Street Arena to broadcast a hockey game on [*Star*-owned] *CFCA* radio! The cub reporter obliged, inventing hockey play-by-play on the fly in a rinkside glass booth. Seeing his first goal, he shouted over the phone to the station, "He shoots, he scores!" The game, an overtime affair between local Parkdale and Kitchener teams, impressed his employers. Hockey became a regular assignment. And within a decade, Hewitt was a household name. In the '40s, he received 90,000 fan letters a year and, according to a survey, was better known than Prime Minister Mackenzie King.

Every broadcast would begin with Charles Jennings' finely sculpted broadcaster's voice: "Your Imperial Oil hockey broadcast," the father of future ABC-TV anchorman Peter Jennings would intone. "… Bringing you *Foster Hewitt!*"

Then came a more insistent cry: "Hello Canada! And hockey fans in the United States and Newfoundland! The score … "

The exclamation marks are crucial. Hewitt's passion for what was to come — the final periods of a game that (in 1939) reached two million listeners, one of five Canadians — was immediately evident. But after his opening salvo, Foster would instinctively calm us (and himself) down. Next he would talk about the weather, and what it was like in Toronto or Montreal that evening.

Novelist Hugh MacLennan observed, "To spectator and player alike, hockey gives the release that strong liquor gives a repressed man. It is," he wrote, "the counterpart of Canadian self-restraint."

In the '30s and '40s, our great national obsession found an ideal interpreter in Foster Hewitt. For even Foster's signature call — "He shoots, he scores!" — was unmistakably Canadian, with its simple, uncluttered phrasing. Yet with the last two words Foster would take leave of his senses with a shout of absolute delirium.

Our most famous voice made Saturday nights synonymous with hockey. And the figure of two million listeners is probably low, for the game was everywhere in the air then. Political pundit Dalton Camp remembered encountering Hewitt's voice while on leave from the army:

I recall walking an empty street in a cold Canadian town on a Saturday night, in the sharp, biting cold, smoke rising from chimneys of huddled, shuttered houses, inside lights dimmed by drawn curtains, and then hearing the voice of Foster Hewitt. … Hearing the unseen but familiar rhythms of the game, the urgent voice, and the sound of the crowd rising and falling as a chorus as practised as any church choir. It was an epiphanous moment and, I have since thought, there has been nothing like it, nothing so unique, in all the entertainment arts in the national memory.

Sportswriter Trent Frayne elaborated on what it was like to be snug inside a home, thrilling to Foster Hewitt's rendition of *Hockey Night in Canada*:

Those of us who grew up in the prairies listening to his voice will never forget [Foster Hewitt] coming over the airwaves and greeting us. "Hello Canada! And hockey fans in the United States and Newfoundland," he'd say. "The score at the end of the first period is …" And then he'd tell us, the millions of us spread right across the country, brought together in living rooms and kitchens and bathtubs and cars and on lonely dark farms and in small snow-packed towns and in big brightly lit cities from one ocean to the other, all of us in our mind's eye watching the matchless giants on the ice below.

A rambunctious early ad for the radio hit, *Hockey Night in Canada*. "Matinee idol" Foster Hewitt is at the microphone (top, middle).

As Our Radio Friends See Us

FIRST GARDENS BROADCAST (AND BOOS)

The 48th Highlanders and Royal Grenadiers strike up "Happy Days Are Here Again!" minutes before the Toronto Maple Leafs take on the Chicago Black Hawks in the opening game of Maple Leaf Gardens.

Near the end of Conn Smythe's strenuous campaign to coax Maple Leaf Gardens to life, the Leaf owner approached radio man Foster Hewitt, who'd cultivated a following broadcasting from the Mutual Street Arena, and asked where he wanted to set up in the new ice palace.

Just as infantrymen dream of being above the fray in the air corps, Hewitt, who regularly froze his feet working ice level at the old Leaf rink, coveted an aerial view of hockey battles. So he visited a store on Bay Street and chugged upstairs in search of the ideal perspective of patrons on the sidewalk below.

The fifth floor — 56 feet up — was perfect, Foster figured. Smythe quickly built a broadcast perch, connected by zigzagging catwalks, to those specifications. C.M. Pasmore, an ad executive connected with Leafs broadcasts, commented, "Why it looks like the gondola on an airship."

The first time Hewitt ventured to his new post, he flew into a panic. The slender, twisting catwalk had no guardrails and Foster was forced to make the last part of his inaugural journey in slow inches on hands and knees.

Once Hewitt crept inside the "gondola," a sparsely furnished box whose walls were decorated with cables, more problems arose. Opening ceremonies dragged on. Military bands marched and played. Then marched and played some more. And few of the attending politicians could pass up an opportunity to address 13,233 voters — at the time the largest crowd to witness a local sports event.

Foster advised listeners that spectators were getting grumpy. Stray boos cascaded down. The mood didn't improve with the game's first goal by Chicago's Mush March. The Black Hawks* went on to win, 2–1. The crowd, who'd paid 75¢ to $2.75 for tickets, left the game mumbling. Radio fans of the Leafs slumped off to bed to wrestle with their pillows.

No matter. There would soon be better games and memories.

*The team was called the Black Hawks up until the mid-80s, and then became the Blackhawks.

MANNA FROM HEAVEN

Conn Smythe talks hockey with King Clancy and Red Horner (right).

Hockey Night in Canada was hatched on a nine-hole summer golf course near Lake Simcoe, Ontario, in June 1929. Leaf owner Conn Smythe and Jack MacLaren, a Toronto ad executive, were on their second way around the course — the sixth hole, a caddie remembered — when the men stopped and shook hands. "It's a deal, I'll have an agreement drawn," MacLaren declared. The suggestion irked Smythe. "You have my word and we shook hands! What more do you need?" With that exchange, Smythe sold rights to hockey games at what would become Maple Leaf Gardens to MacLaren and his client, General Motors. The first Leaf broadcasts aired on three local stations. But by early 1933, a 20-station hookup relayed broadcasts in English from both Toronto and Montreal. In 1936, Imperial Oil (another MacLaren client) replaced GM as sponsor. On January 1, 1937, the Canadian Broadcasting Corporation (CBC) was launched and assumed national carriage of HNIC. Vinegary Smythe would later say of his first broadcast deal, "When Jack MacLaren suggested we would get money for hockey broadcasts, it was then I believed the story about manna from heaven."

The Kid Line — Charlie Conacher, Joe Primeau and Harvey "Busher" Jackson — catapulted the Leafs to their first Stanley Cup in 1932. The finals were best three-of-five back then. And the Kids went to work on the Bill and Bun Cook-Frank Boucher edition of the New York Rangers early, with Jackson firing a hat trick in a 6–4 opening game. The second game (held in Boston because the circus invaded Madison Square Garden) again went

Golden Leafs. First row, left-right: Tim Daly (trainer), Frank Selke, Sr., Hap Day (captain), Conn Smythe and coach Dick Irvin, Sr. Charlie Conacher is second from the left in the middle row; linemate Busher Jackson is four players over, next to goalie, Lorne Chabot. And that's King Clancy top, left. Look how small the Stanley Cup was back then!

to Toronto, 6–2, with Conacher and Jackson scoring and Primeau setting up King Clancy and future Hot Stove regular, Baldy Cotton. Back home for game three, Conacher literally put a bullet through the Rangers' heart when, with his team up 3–1, he let go a missile from just inside the New York blueline that caught netminder John Ross Roach in the chest. The goalie fell to the ice, struggling for breath, then rose five minutes later, shaken, to let in two quick goals, giving Toronto a 6–4 victory and the championship.

Toronto's fabled Kid Line: Charlie Conacher, Joe Primeau and Harvey Jackson. All three earned the maximum $7,000-a-year salary at a time when the Depression-plagued NHL enforced a $62,000 team salary cap.

The first stars of hockey's radio era were three Leaf skaters — Charlie Conacher, Harvey Jackson and Joe Primeau — who earned Foster Hewitt's (and therefore Canada's) fancy while picking up the first perk of sports stardom: colourful nicknames.

"The Kid Line" was a tonic against the Depression — the boldest, most creative forward unit to ever don Leaf blue. Jackson was a magical skater with a deft scoring touch; Conacher, a freight train with a powerful shot; Primeau, in the middle, a peerless playmaker.

The trio placed at the top of NHL scoring the season Maple Leaf Gardens opened, tallying 75 goals in 48 games during the 1931–32 campaign. That Jackson and Conacher were local boys, while Primeau hailed from nearby Lindsay, made them instantly popular with a Gardens crowd hungry for fresh heroes.

It must be said the boys didn't shy from success. Jackson earned his nickname as a rookie just up from the Marlies in 1929. "Help me carry these sticks to the players' box," trainer Tim Daly asked him. "Carry them yourself," the 19-year-old snorted. "Well, I'll be a son of a bitch if you ain't one smart busher," Daly replied. From then on, the hockey player was "Busher" Jackson.

Conacher went by "Big Chas" or "The Big Bomber." And he was even less likely to entertain unwelcome requests. Legend has it the powerful (6'1", 195 pounds) forward was out for a skate one practice and heard team owner and legendary martinet Conn Smythe bellow out a critique of Conacher's play.

Conacher drifted toward the boards and hoisted a stick at his employer. "One more crack like that," he promised, "and I'll whack your &#*$ head off!"

In the midst of such rowdy company, it's no surprise the placid Primeau earned a more dignified moniker. Fans and reporters inevitably referred to "Busher's" and "Big Chas's" linemate as "Gentleman Joe" Primeau.

THE KITCHENER CONNECTION

After the Kid Line, the next great trio to make it to the NHL was the Kraut Line — Bobby Bauer, Milt Schmidt and Woodrow Wilson "Porky" Dumart — Boston's Kitchener Connection. The trio came 1-2-3 in scoring in the 1939–40 season. Two campaigns later, the players would all be serving in the RCAF. Fellow NHLer and future HNIC analyst Bob Goldham would later say, when asked to rank NHL centres, "You can have Jean Beliveau and Wayne Gretzky and the rest — none of them were all-out like Schmidt. He didn't need a bodyguard; he took care of himself."

The Kraut Line (left-right): Bobby Bauer, Milt Schmidt and Woody Dumart. All were born in or around Kitchener (formerly Berlin), Ontario. Early in the 20th century, German was heard as often as English at area rinks.

THEY SHOOT BUT NEVER SCORE April 3–4, 1933

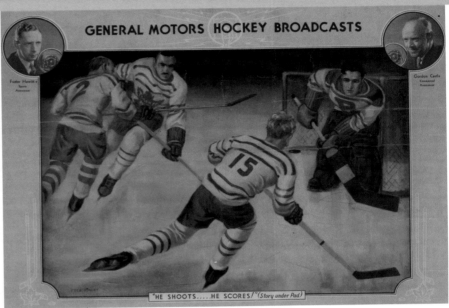

GENERAL MOTORS HOCKEY BROADCASTS

"HE SHOOTS.....HE SCORES!" (Story under Pad)

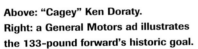

Above: "Cagey" Ken Doraty.
Right: a General Motors ad illustrates the 133-pound forward's historic goal.

HNIC's first great overtime rivalled Depression-era dance marathons for drama and difficulty. It was the deciding fifth game of the Boston-Toronto semis. Three preceding games went overtime, so no one was surprised when regular play ended at a scoreless draw.

Nothing changed in the next three extra frames. Drooping fans left the Gardens in search of bed. But more listeners took their place, drawn by the word that Leafs were letting everyone in free.

During the fourth overtime, King Clancy slipped one past Bruin "twine-tender" Tiny Thompson. But wait, a whistle had blown. No goal. Between periods, Foster received notes on how players were doing. Hearing athletes were lying in dressing rooms, Hewitt sighed, "I wouldn't mind doing the same."

Soon Foster's vision blurred. Then he fell silent. A colleague raced into the booth to find Foster completely out, teetering backward.

Next intermission, NHL president Frank Calder asked teams to flip a coin or play without goaltenders. No wash.

Early in the sixth overtime, a revived Foster Hewitt caught the scent of impending drama:

"There's Eddie Shore going for the puck in the corner beside the Boston net! Andy Blair is on for the Leafs now — he hasn't played as much as the others and seems a little fresher than some. He's moving in on Shore in the corner. Shore is clearing the puck ... *Blair intercepts! Blair has the puck! Ken Doraty is dashing for the net! Blair passes! Doraty takes it! He shoots! He scores!*"

The intimacy of radio and Foster Hewitt's stirring rendition of Toronto games made support for the Maple Leafs a welcome civic duty through much of Canada during the Depression.

This national condition became evident in the final month of 1933 when Toronto travelled to play archrival Boston. (The teams met in the playoffs five times from 1933–39.)

With Toronto leading in the second period, Leaf forward Ace Bailey, a consummate stickhandler, foiled a Bruin power play with a fancy solo dash, enraging Boston star Eddie Shore. Regaining the puck, Shore made for the Leaf net, but was chopped down by King Clancy.

When Shore lifted himself up, his eyes were lime pits of fury. Finding Bailey with his back turned, the charging Bruin accelerated, dipped his shoulder and caught Bailey in the

Irvine "Ace" Bailey shortly after his controversial injury. Bailey led the NHL in goals (22) and points (32) in the 1928–29 season.

kidneys, sending him over his shoulder. (Some believe Shore, blinded by rage, thought he was attacking Clancy.)

According to a reporter close to Hewitt, the sound of Bailey's head hitting ice was "like a pumpkin being cracked by a baseball bat." In the dressing room afterward, a doctor stood over the shaking Leaf and said, "If this boy is Roman Catholic, we should call a priest." Later, Shore visited Bailey. "It's OK, Eddie," Bailey told him, "I guess it's all part of the game." Then he fell into a coma.

Bailey's battle to survive played out on the front pages of Canadian newspapers. Editorialists cried out for revenge. Bailey's dad bought a gun and travelled to Boston for Shore, but was intercepted by police. Two weeks and as many operations later, Bailey recovered, but never played again.

HNIC's Foster Hewitt would later comment, "The incident made me understand the power of our broadcasts. Everyone in Canada seemed to think Ace … was a boy from their town."

A *Toronto Star* photographic account of the grim aftermath of the Bailey-Shore incident. In the first photo, Red Horner finds his distressed teammate. Moments later, Horner approached Shore, asking, "What you do that for, Eddie?" When Shore smirked, Horner knocked him out with a single punch. In the third photo, Shore is being assisted off the ice.

The movie camera's eye caught several scenes during the now historic Shore ha uin-Leaf game in Boston. Here are three pictures taken shortly after is far fr iley was crashed to the ice and Shore was knocked out by Horner. with his

STAR–DEC.16 1933 ②

MOVIE CAMERA PRESERVES SCENES OF HISTORIC BOSTON B

istoric Shore have both been suspended for their part in the fracas. Shore himself rink. Two of the Leafs are down on th after is far from feeling fit. In the first picture Bailey is lying on the ice Smythe can be seen making his way rner with his team-mates gathered round him. Horner is seen looking down at his the players are scattered all over th ation injured pal. The

C BOSTON BRAWL

THE FIRST ALL-STAR GAME March 6, 1934

The NHL dealt with the Shore-Bailey incident by suspending Shore for 16 games and decreeing that an all-star benefit would take place on behalf of the fallen Leaf star.

That game, pitting Toronto against stars of the eight remaining NHL teams, including future Hall-of-Famers Shore, Howie Morenz, Aurel Joliet and Lionel Conacher, took place at Maple Leaf Gardens two months after Bailey's injury, with the home-town team winning, 7–3.

The game's climax came before the puck dropped when Shore and Bailey met for the first time since the injury. As Foster Hewitt recounted, more than 14,000 roared in thunderous approval as "Shore and Bailey looked at each other for a moment, then clasped hands and talked quietly."

Above: the NHL's very first all stars. Eddie Shore, fourth from left, top row. Howie Morenz is fourth from the right, second row. Right, below: Eddie Shore and Ace Bailey (centre) let bygones be begones. Foster Hewitt (far left) conducts pre-game ceremony.

Alfie Moore played 21 seasons, mostly in the minors.

Many hockey players have replenished lost fluids after a game at a bar. Alfie Moore was in a pub drinking *before* the biggest game of his life.

The Black Hawks were in Toronto with a big playoff game and no goalie. Mike Karakas was hurt. And Conn Smythe wouldn't allow Chicago to use Ranger goalie Dave Kerr, a Toronto native. The only other local goalie coach Bill Stewart knew of was Moore. At a team meeting he asked if anyone knew where the minor leaguer could be found. Someone dryly suggested checking out the bars. Indeed, a search party located Moore at a nearby tavern. The goalie had been there awhile, so it took a few coffees to rinse him free of suds.

Stewart advised his Hawks to take it easy on the goalie during practice. "Don't want him hurt," the coach said, eyeing his fill-in with evident regret. At first, Stewart's fear seemed well placed. Moore fanned on his first shot. But seeing the disappointment in his teammates' eyes strengthened the career minor leaguer's resolve. After that, he became invincible, turning back every Leaf attack. As he left the team, Moore was asked how much he wanted for one night of work. "Would $150 be reasonable?" he inquired. The Hawks paid him $300 and put his name on the Stanley Cup.

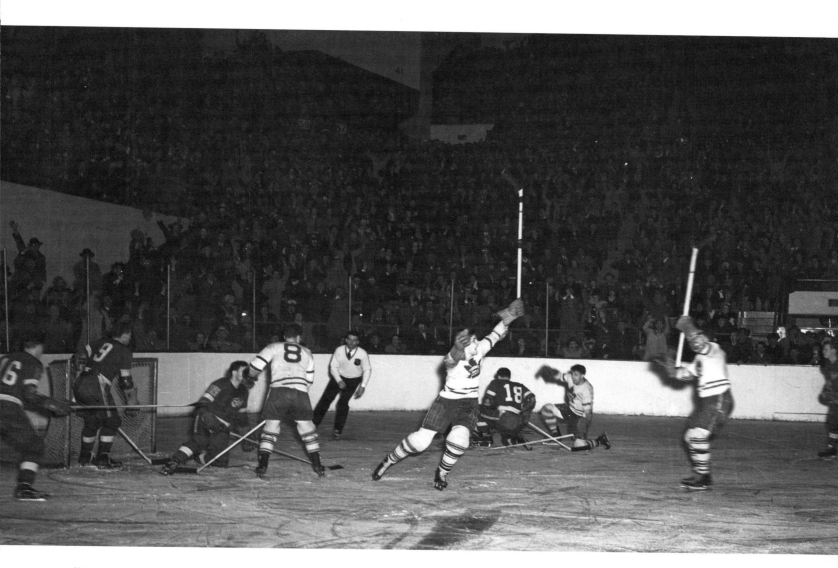

Hooray! Leafs celebrate a goal against the Red Wings. Detroit netminder Johnny Mowers is hidden behind teammate Pat McCreavy (18). Yes, there was a number nine in Detroit before Gordie Howe. That's Mud Bruneteau stationed in front of the Red Wing net.

Toronto and New York were the class of the NHL in the 1941–42 season. And after the Leafs dispensed with the Rangers in the semis, thanks to the great play of chunky netminder Turk Broda and frequent creasemate Bucko McDonald — "They used two goaltenders against us," Frank Boucher moaned — Hap Day's boys looked to be a cinch in the finals. The green, grabby Wings were "young hooligans," coach Day sniffed. Nevertheless, the upstarts jumped to a three-game lead and appeared on the verge

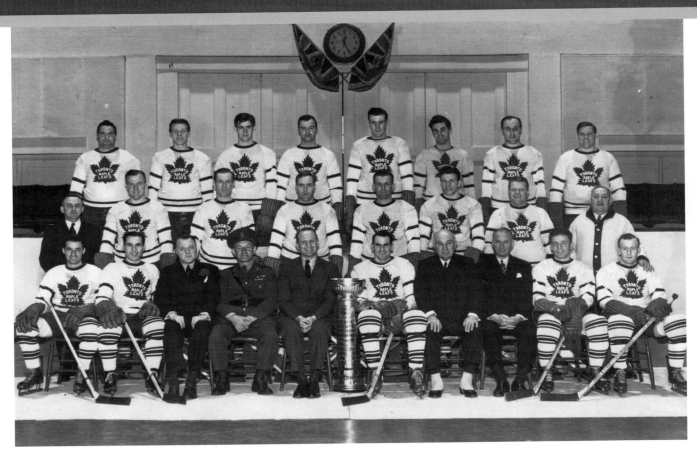

of an upset. So Day resorted to shameless psychological manipulation, pinning onto the team bulletin board a letter from a 14-year-old schoolgirl who prayed the Leafs could come back. They did, with Sweeney Schriner leading the team to four straight wins. Perhaps there was a divine hand in the never-equalled comeback. Certainly, the Wings fell victim to their churlish ways, losing GM coach Jack Adams to a suspension in the pivotal fourth game when he slid across the ice after the game to bop referee Mel Harwood in the snout.

"Major" Conn Smythe, fourth from left, bottom row, and the champion 1941–42 Toronto Maple Leafs. Coach Hap Day and captain Syl Apps are to Smythe's immediate right. Well-upholstered goalie Turk Broda is second from the end, far right, middle row.

ENVOYEZ, MAURICE

March 23, 1944

A young Rocket Richard scores his 100th goal against Turk Broda at Maple Leaf Gardens.

Winters growing up, Maurice Richard played hockey all day, eating supper with skates on so he could hurry back to the rink. After a junior and minor league career marked by injuries, he willed his way onto the Canadiens in 1942. Coach Dick Irvin said he never encountered a player with a greater need to succeed. Richard's first NHL season was ruined by injuries, but in 1943–44, Maurice became the Rocket, electrifying Forum fans playing right wing (while shooting left) on a line with Elmer Lach and Toe Blake. Seeing the Rocket bear down on a goalie, eyes glowing as if he'd swallowed a candle, Montreal fans called out, *"Envoyez, Maurice!"* In the playoffs, Maurice was unstoppable, scoring 12 goals in nine games, including five against Paul Bibeault in Toronto. Afterward, Elmer Ferguson acknowledged the Rocket's performance:

" … And the first star, Rocket Richard. Second star, Rocket Richard. … And the third star — Rocket Richard."

How fierce was the Montreal-Toronto rivalry? One night in Toronto, Habs' Toe Blake couldn't find socks after the game, so sent a clubhouse boy in search of something for his feet. When the kid came back carrying white hose with blue leaf trim, Toe exploded, shouting, "I'd rather freeze," and then stormed sockless into the freezing winter night. Toe and the Rocket went on to defeat the Leafs in the 1944 semi-finals on their way to win the Stanley Cup. Toronto, behind goalie Frank McCool, surprised Montreal in 1945 en route to a championship. Montreal won the next year and seemed on the verge of taking Toronto in the '47 finals,

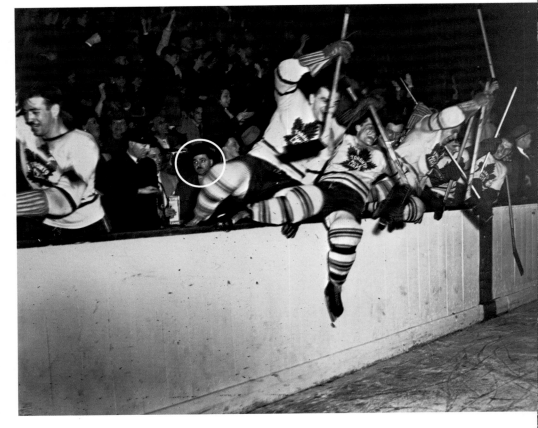

Leafs blow off the bench to celebrate Stanley Cup win. Mustached Garth Boesch decides to use the gate while Harry Watson and Bill Ezinicki scramble over the boards. Glum Montreal publicity director Camil des Roches (circled) was on his way to make the team's travel arrangements.

jumping to a 6–0 first game victory. But then the Leafs, led by youngsters Howie Meeker and Bill Barilko, rebounded for a six-game win. The accompanying image is worth a thousand Montreal-Toronto game accounts from the period. The lone sad face in the shot — a picture of the Leafs leaping to the ice after taking the Cup — is Montreal publicity director Camil des Roches. The Habs' official was on his way to discuss travel arrangements with a railway official, who had seats behind the Leafs bench. Des Roches was particularly glum, he later told HNIC's Ward Cornell, because seconds earlier Toe Blake had been foiled on a breakaway by Turk Broda. Harry "Whipper" Watson and Bill Ezinicki are leading the charge over the Leafs bench.

OTHER "CANADIAN TEAM" GETS SCARE March 28, 1950

The other "Canadian team" from hockey's golden era would be the Detroit Red Wings, who forged crucial junior affiliations with Edmonton and Guelph in the '40s, and took advantage of an NHL rule allowing clubs to protect players born within a 50-mile radius (giving Detroit more than a few southern Ontario skaters).

From out West came Gordie Howe (Floral, Saskatchewan) and Terry Sawchuk (Winnipeg). In 1950, Ontario recruits included "Terrible" Ted Lindsay, Red Kelly and rookie Alex Delvecchio. Though Detroit dominated the regular season, their first opponents in the post season were Toronto, a team they'd lost to in the playoffs four of five previous springs.

The Leaf "hex" seemed real in the first game of the playoffs when Gordie Howe checked Teeder Kennedy, stumbled, and fell in a grotesque tangle into the boards. When he didn't get up, a sickly hush fell over Detroit's Olympia — a palpable gloom that could be felt by HNIC radio listeners in living rooms and kitchens all across Canada. Gordie later required a 90-minute operation on his skull to save his life, and never played in the remainder of the playoffs. The Wings would go on to win the Cup, but years later, Howe would remark, "I know we won four Stanley Cups, but I have no memory of anything that happened that first win."

Gordie Howe in his prime. The ambidextrous winger used a straight blade so he could shoot from both the left and right sides.

WORST MOVIE CRITIC, BEST GOALIE April 15, 1952

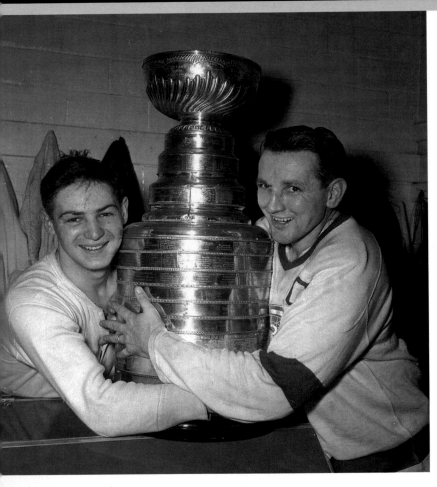

A fresh-faced, jubilant Terry Sawchuk hugs his first Stanley Cup.
Beside him, captain Sid Abel enjoys his last appearance in a Red
Wing uniform.

When he was on, goalie Terry Sawchuk was a magician who could make the net behind him disappear. As a child growing up in Winnipeg, Terry didn't tax his eyes. He wouldn't go to movies and he laid off reading in winter. Vision, he told himself (and presumably his schoolteachers), was something to be used in the stopping of speeding rubber. In the 1952 playoffs, Sawchuk stopped everything he saw at home, recording four shutouts in an eight-game sweep of Toronto and Montreal. (Perhaps because it seemed as if Sawchuk had the use of eight arms to block opponents' shots, Detroit fans started tossing octopuses onto the ice that playoff season.)

THE MYSTERY OF BILL BARILKO April 21, 1951

"Bill Barilko disappeared that summer, he was on a fishing trip.
The last goal he ever scored won the Leafs the Cup ..."

Tragically Hip — "50 Mission Cap"

Bill Barilko was a bashing defender who played hockey with contagious joy. And unlike most blue-liners of the era, Bill occasionally jumped to offence in the opposition zone, hungry for rebounds.

Still, Bill seemed to come out of nowhere in what would be the defining moment of the 1951 Stanley Cup finals. Toronto was leading Montreal three games to one, but barely managed to send the fifth game into overtime with a scrambling last-minute goal by Tod Sloan. (Incredibly, every game in the series went into OT.)

In that final extra session, beyond-tense HNIC fans listened as Howie Meeker liberated the puck behind the Montreal net, and then fired a blind backhand to linemate Harry Watson, who slapped the puck off Butch Bouchard's skate. No camera caught Barilko's shot. On game film, he just appeared in the top-left corner of the screen, falling, following through on a backhand. (Written reports suggest it was a slapshot.) In any case, the puck travelled over goalie Gerry McNeil. And the Leafs won their seventh Stanley Cup.

"I don't know where Barilko came from," McNeil said later.

No one knew for sure why Barilko had fallen. Film from the dressing room later shows a jubilant

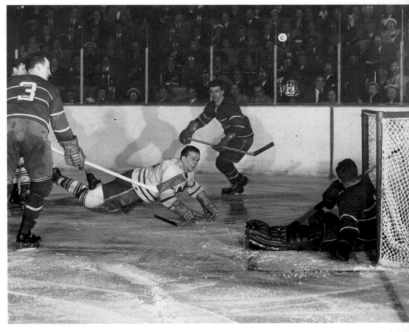

Two perspectives of the most famous goal in Maple Leaf history.

Barilko getting an affectionate cuffing around from teammates. He was 24 years old, the picture of health.

That summer Barilko was returning to his Timmins home from a fishing trip, when his single-engine plane, piloted by a friend, disappeared. Search efforts proved fruitless. But teammates refused to believe he was gone. Bill's equipment remained in his old stall at Maple Leaf Gardens the following fall.

The Leafs would not win another Stanley Cup until the spring of 1962. Coincidentally, two months later, Barilko's plane was finally discovered north of Cochrane, Ontario.

Bill Barilko, still flush with victory, moments after his Stanley Cup-winning goal. Shortly after this photograph was taken, Leaf President Conn Smythe approached Barilko, feigning outrage at how the defenceman had left his position.

ROYAL WINTER FAIR

In 1951, the Toronto Maple Leafs played the Black Hawks in a special one-hour, watch-the-swearing, lay-off-the-rough-stuff, afternoon exhibition match for a visiting Princess. The two teams would be their usual expressive selves later in the evening for the regular HNIC radio broadcast. Here Teeder Kennedy greets the Princess in a pre-game ceremony. Leaf owner Conn Smythe handles the introductions. Prince Philip looks on.

Princess Elizabeth at Maple Leaf Gardens. She also visited the Montreal Forum during the 1951 royal tour. Many Canadians bought their first televisions in 1953 to watch Elizabeth's coronation.

For some hockey fans, the advent of TV was an unsettling pleasure. Yes, it was great finally seeing games live. But the heroics of certain players played better in our imaginations than on cramped, black-and-white screens.

Joseph-Henri-Maurice the "Rocket" Richard was a figure of worship in Montreal. He also enjoyed an unrivalled dramatic flair. It comes as no surprise that he provided the last great moment in hockey's radio era.

The game in question occurred in the spring of 1952. Montreal was battling Boston in the seventh game of the semi-finals. Early on, Richard was waylaid by a murderous check and spent two periods battling consciousness.

With minutes left in a one-all game, a climbing expectancy in the crowd's voice called Richard to battle. Returning to a hero's welcome, the Rocket gathered the puck behind his net, his eyes alive with purpose. Swinging by a checker, he exploded up the wing, and then, fuelled by the Forum's roar, flew by another Bruin at centre ice.

Veering toward the boards, Richard was met by another Boston defender, whom he threw aside with a swimmer's backstroke. Finally, Boston goalie Sugar Jim Henry raced out, risking

Sugar Jim Henry pays homage to Rocket Richard shortly after the Rocket's greatest goal. Henry himself was recovering from a head injury suffered earlier in the playoffs. Portrait by artist Geri Storey.

a poke check. Richard swerved, drew the puck back and fired home the game and series winner, sending the Canadien nation, both in the Forum and at home listening to the game on radio, into pandemonium.

Minutes later, in the dressing room, Richard broke into sobbing convulsions and was put under heavy sedation.

KEEPING WARM
BETWEEN PERIODS

Though NHL hockey was an immediate radio hit, no one could figure out what to do during intermissions.

Early on, games were interrupted by between-period musical interludes, as genteel emcee John Holden would throw to the Joe de Courcy or Luigi Romanelli bands at the Silver Slipper dance hall — "and now, for your dancing pleasure …"

— in what was a clear invitation for listeners to hit the fridge for a snack.

Then in 1939, C.M. Pasmore — the MacLaren's executive who named the "gondola" — came up with the "Hot Stove League," where scribes Elmer "Fergy" Ferguson, Bobby Hewitson, Wes McKnight and former player "Baldy" Cotton gabbed about hockey in a studio near the Leafs dressing room.

Because it was wartime, the exchanges were scripted, as was all radio at the time. (Censors reviewed scripts for material that might give away military secrets.)

Nevertheless, the boys frequently departed from script. Baldy Cotton once got so worked up, he failed to see his sleeve catch fire from a flaming coffee cup full of discarded cigar butts.

The Hot Stove League was a regular part of early HNIC-TV telecasts. A country store set was constructed, where regulars, including retired Leafs Teeder Kennedy and Syl Apps, pretended to tend the stove. Baldy Cotton, who ordinarily wore a suit, was now decked out in work duds, to further encourage a homey ambiance. But somehow it wasn't the same. Maybe because the set was in CBC's Jarvis Street studio, around the corner from Maple Leaf Gardens.

At the beginning of the 1957–58 season, the Hot Stove League was replaced by an intermission host. The concept was revived, however, with great success, in the '90s, when Ron MacLean began hosting a bustling, cross-continent "Satellite Hotstove."

Author-journalist Jack Batten once captured his youthful enthusiasm for the radio "Hot Stove League" in a piece for the now defunct *Canadian Magazine*:

The Hot Stove League is in session. Front row, seated (left to right): "Baldy" Cotton, Wes McKnight, Bobby Hewitson and Elmer Ferguson. Standing: Dave Price, Murray Westgate and Syl Apps.

The men of the "Hot Stove League" seemed wiser than members of [Prime Minister] Mackenzie King's cabinet: Bobby Hewitson, the chirpy little sports editor of the *Toronto Telegram*; Elmer Ferguson from Montreal, heavy with years and erudition; lovable Harold Cotton, a scout for the Boston Bruins. Wes McKnight was the moderator — impartial, even kind of distant. ... We didn't mind the fuss Fergy went through when he named the three stars at the end of each game. Why three stars, by the way? why not two? or four? Because Imperial happened to peddle a brand of gasoline called Three Star.

THE GOOD OL' DAYS

Like many other hockey-mad Canadians living in the thirties and forties, I grew up with Foster Hewitt and the Maple Leafs Kid Line. Later we had Turk Broda, Syl Apps and Gordie Drillon. And after that, "The Whirling Dirvish" Wally Stanowski, Frank McCool and Teeder Kennedy.

At the same time, Charlie Harwood was the English voice of the Montreal Maroons and J. Arthur Dupont spun the tales of the colourful Canadiens *"en français."*

All of them came to us on CBC Radio — magical voices taking us on Saturday night trips to Maple Leaf Gardens or the Montreal Forum, verbal voyages that let our imaginations run wild. And what adventures they were as we pictured ourselves cheering a Charlie Conacher breakaway or a spectacular Wilf Cude save. When the reality of television came into our homes in the autumn of 1952, "hockey" as we knew it, changed forever.

Yes, time marches on and change is inevitable. Gone too are CBC Radio's other broadcast icons, Danny Gallivan, Fred Sgambati and Dan Kelly, leaving only Bob Cole whose play-by-play career began on CBC Radio. Somehow there's never been anything quite like those early calls — *"He shoots! He scores!"* — to stir the soul, delivering delirious joy or devastating disaster.

Those indeed were the good old days — sadly never to be heard again. **Frank Selke, Jr.**

Frank Selke, Jr., interviews Saskatchewan-born rivals and off-season fishing pals Gordie Howe and Johnny Bower on the ice moments after Toronto took the Stanley Cup in 1963.

The *Hockey Night in Canada Theme*, or "Canada's Second National Anthem" as it is affectionately known, was composed by Dolores Claman. It was first recorded for broadcast in 1968 and today remains one of the longest-running themes in broadcasting history. Over the years, it has undergone different arrangements. It has been arranged for high school bands, and two piano arrangements are included as part of the graded Royal Conservatory of Music repertoire.

This song and the phrase "Happy Motoring" became synonymous with *Hockey Night in Canada* and a smiling Murray Westgate for a whole generation of Canadians. Today, the music is proudly displayed as part of the Esso Archives.

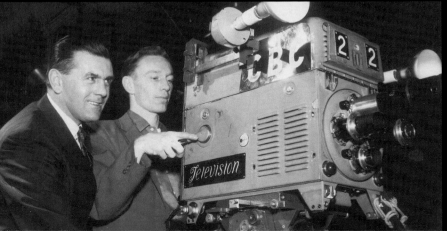

MONSIEUR HOCKEY

Bow-tied René Lecavalier follows play in a game at the Forum.

The first man to ever broadcast a hockey game on television and the voice of the Montreal Canadiens for more than 30 years, René Lecavalier can be considered one of the great Canadian educators of the twentieth century.

In Quebec, he is widely credited with having done more to preserve the quality of spoken French than a dozen education reforms. Before Lecavalier, a former radio war correspondent and cultural commentator, found his way to the Montreal Forum, French hockey terminology was mostly borrowed English.

The dapper, mustached Lecavalier changed all that, introducing terms — *la rondelle* instead of *puck*, for instance — that quickly found their way into Quebec culture. Radio-Canada coverage of the Canadiens also spilled into other provinces, where English Montreal fans would abandon the Leafs for René's coverage of the Habs. So it could also be said that Lecavalier taught two generations of Canadiens English fans how to speak hockey in French.

In Quebec, French and English kids alike enjoyed mimicking his elegant diction while playing street hockey. (*"Rousseau avec la rondelle. Il lance! Il compte! Oh, bravo, Monsieur Rousseau!"*) And French-Canadian comedian-impersonator André-Philippe Gagnon had a wonderful routine where the impeccably professional Lecavalier interviewed loutish, barely articulate players.

Like all great broadcasters, Lecavalier was a brilliant storyteller whose images stayed with the viewer long after the story ended. At his funeral, in 1999, Jean Beliveau commented, "He would describe what was happening and for days afterward the people would still see it in their minds."

THE THREE BEST SEATS
IN THE HOUSE

Early September 1952, Montreal — I am 24 years old. Four months earlier, I was a print journalist. I loved it. Now I am employed as a TV sports' producer at Radio-Canada. I have a delicate assignment. I have to meet the brass of the Montreal Canadiens at the hallowed Forum, home of Maurice Richard and his adoring fans.

What am I to do? What kind of reception awaits me? The meeting is set by representatives of MacLaren advertising, the holder of radio and television rights. I have no textbooks as a reference on "How to Televise" a hockey game. I am wracking my brain, hoping for some kind of inspiration, some kind of flash. I am constantly thinking of camera locations and functions. I have to submit concrete proposals to the Canadiens brass. Then bravo! I have a flash.

I will try to obtain for TV viewers — fewer than 20,000 in the fall of 1952 — THE BEST SEAT in the house. Sounds logical to me. Armed with this basic principle, I was able to obtain three reliable camera positions after discussions with the Canadiens representatives, VP Kenny Reardon, Camil des Roches and Frank Selke, Sr.

It might seem amusing that such a flimsy flash should be so important to me. Yet, the success of getting the best seat in the house for the viewer allowed me to pursue a flourishing career as a TV producer for 36 years.

Who knows what would have happened without this flash?

Gérald Renaud

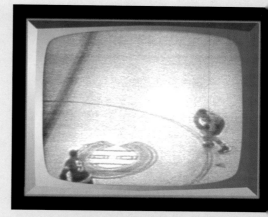

Top: Detroit's Gordie Howe intercepts a pass from Montreal's Elmer Lach at centre ice.
Bottom: six Hockey Hall of Famers in action during the first-ever *HNIC* TV broadcast — Bert Olmstead (15), Red Kelly (4), Gordie Howe (9) and Rocket Richard (9). Terry Sawchuk and Ted Lindsay collide beside the Detroit net.

BLUE AND RED IN BLACK AND WHITE October 11, 1952

Above, top: a cameraman follows the action from Maple Leaf Gardens in the first year of televised hockey. Below: Leaf forward Sid Smith looks for rebound off Bruin goalie "Sugar" Jim Henry in action from the very first televised game from Maple Leaf Gardens.

The first HNIC image to appear on television was a closeup of the Montreal Canadiens crest at centre ice in the old Forum. Producer Gérald Renaud then cut to the stands — men in fedoras and women wearing furs — before moving to the faceoff. Finally, play-by-play-man René Lecavalier greeted viewers with a cheery, "*Bonsoir, mesdames et messieurs ...*" The puck was then dropped and sent back to Detroit's number nine.

"*Howe est le premier à toucher la rondelle ...*"

Montreal was first to host an HNIC broadcast. And though scant footage exists of that first game, a version of the November 1st, 1952, match between Montreal and New York has been preserved. (The first Leafs HNIC contest, between Toronto and Boston, with Foster Hewitt at the mike, took place that same Saturday.)

The November 1st Montreal HNIC contest makes for fascinating viewing. There is no music, no ads on the boards, no commercial interruptions. Nor are there any faceoff circles — just demure beauty marks to the left and right of the goal.

Also, players seem to take professional pride in not going offside or icing the puck.

There are almost no breaks. Or talking, really. Lecavalier is sparing in his comments.

All there is, is hockey. And, most of all, Rocket Richard. Though this isn't Richard's best game, the camera follows him around like an adoring kid brother. Even during faceoffs, the camera is on the gum-chewing right-winger.

Television was an immediate hit in Canada. Though sets cost $429 at the time (and the average working man earned $3,500 a year), stores couldn't keep enough sets in stock in the fall and winter of 1952–53.

And *HNIC* — the Saturday night broadcast of the Toronto Blue and Montreal Red — in glorious black and white, quickly became one of Canada's first TV hits. A 1955 news story reported a besieged retailer in Rimouski, Quebec, snowmobiling TVs to snowbound customers prior to the Montreal-Detroit Stanley Cup finals.

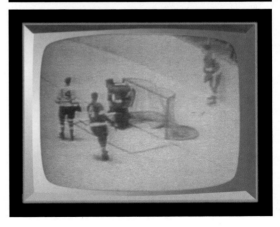

Left: part of a pocket hockey schedule. Top right: CBC station identification (Channel 9 Toronto) prior to first hockey telecast from Maple Leaf Gardens. This telecast was orchestrated by legendary *HNIC* television producer and TV sports pioneer, George Retzlaff. Centre right: Foster Hewitt. Bottom right: action from a November 8, 1952, game between Toronto and Detroit.

V I D E O   A U D I O

BLANK   "It's Hockey Night in Canada".

ESSO ANIMATED JINGLE

FILM CLIP OF HEWITT   On behalf of your neighbourhood Imperial
SUPER CARDS   Esso Dealer, Imperial Oil presents
                                Hockey Night in Canada.

                                Tonight, Toronto Maple Leafs and
                                Montreal Canadiens.

"PLAY-BY-PLAY BY   Play-by-play by Foster Hewitt.
   FOSTER HEWITT"

TO ICE
(SUPER SCORE)

S E C O N D   P E R I O D

V I D E O   A U D I O

STATION BREAK #1 . . . BREAK GIVEN AS SOON AS POSSIBLE AFTER QUARTER HOUR

                                HEWITT SAYS: Now, while the teams are
                                changing players, there'll be a brief
                                pause for station identification (PAUSE)

                                (CUT HEWITT'S AUDIO IN MOBILE UNIT)

SUPER STATION BREAK FROM STUDIO

                                ANNOUNCER: This is your Imperial Esso
                                Hockey Telecast . . . . . For Happy
                                Motoring all winter long, stop at the
                                Imperial Esso Sign.

                                This is CBLT . . . Channel 9 . . .
                                Toronto.

                                (CUT IN HEWITT FOR REMAINDER OF PERIOD)

V I D E O

A U D I O

DISSOLVE FROM ICE TO OLD
RADIO. PULL BACK FAST TO SHOT
OF MURRAY AT COUNTER HOLDING
A RECORD, PLACING IT ON PORT-
ABLE TURNTABLE AND POINTING
TO THE RECORD THEN STARTING
THE MACHINE.

RICK: Well, it looks like our Imperial
Esso Dealer is performing another
experiment . . . he's got a record player
and some special kind of recording ...
wonder what he's going to do . . . oh
well, let's have a look at his audience.
There's Dave Price . . . Hal Cotton . . .
Syl Apps . . . and the Captain of the
Maple Leafs, Ted Kennedy . . . They
all seem pretty interested, too . . .

PULL BACK TO SHOW HOT STOVERS

ALL LOOKING AT MURRAY WITH
INTEREST

MURRAY: Well, that's it fellows . . .
this is sort of a "What's My Name"
contest . . . I'm going to play this
recording and I want you to tell me
who does the talking . . . O.K.?

ALL: OK . . . all set . . .

PLAY DISC

SOUND: DISC OF FOSTER DOING WEATHER
REPORT . . .

MURRAY: How about it fellows, do you
know who it is?

V I D E O

A U D I O

(DAVE PADS FOR 10 SECONDS BEFORE GIVING
3 STARS, ONE AT A TIME, IN SAME ORDER AS
RECEIVED FROM MOBILE TRUCK)

(DAVE PADS FOR 10 TO 12 SECONDS BEFORE
GIVING SHOTS ON GOAL, FINAL SCORE,
OTHER GAMES, AND LEAGUE STANDINGS, AND
CLOSES WITH):

That's it for tonight. We'll be back
next Saturday night with another Hot
Stove League and the game between
Toronto Maple Leafs and Boston Bruins.

(BACK TO MURRAY FOR SIGN-OFF AS FOLLOWS):

On behalf of your neighbourhood Imperial
Esso Dealer, Imperial Oil has presented
Hockey Night in Canada (THEME)

DISSOLVE TO ESSO OVAL

Next Saturday, the Boston Bruins will be
visitors on Toronto ice . . . until then
. . . Goodnight! . . . . . and Happy
Motoring.

CREDITS

T H E M E

OUR FRIENDLY ESSO DEALER

Murray Westgate in uniform. The Toronto actor had a featured role in a second CBC hit, playing from 1980–86 in the comedy-drama *Seeing Things*.

Regina-born Murray Westgate caught the acting bug in high school and scuffled in the Vancouver theatre scene after the war before heading to Toronto because, "If you want to grow strawberries, you go where they grow them."

Early jobs included radio acting and modelling. Then came a fateful industrial film assignment.

"It was an Imperial Oil promotion film," Westgate recalls. "I played a smiling, nicely dressed gas station dealer on one side of the street. Another fellow played the bad dealer across the way. He was a slob, with no customers. They showed this film to gas station dealers at conventions."

A few weeks before HNIC's first Toronto broadcast, the show was still having trouble finding an actor to play an Imperial Oil dealer. "Someone at Imperial said, 'Why don't you use this bird we've been using in our films?'" the retired actor laughs. "And that's how I got the job. Did it for 16 years. When we did commercials live, I'd work one week in Montreal, next one in Toronto."

Westgate rehearsed three hours before each show for his part, which included commercials, Hot Stove League lead ins, and the post-game sign-off.

Not everybody realized he was an actor. "Gosh no," he chuckles. "Can't tell you how many times a stranger asked me to have a look at their car."

Prairie hockey players were supposed to be strapping hulks, so when Conn Smythe first saw featherweight Saskatchewan forward Elmer Lach at a 1938 Leaf tryout camp, a snarl crossed his face. "Too small," he rasped. Two years later, Saskatchewan native Dick Irvin, Sr., took over the Canadiens and brought Lach to Montreal, where he centred the fabulous Punch line with Toe Blake and Rocket Richard. Two scoring championships later, in 1953, he settled the first TV *HNIC* Stanley Cup final, intercepting a Milt Schmidt clearing pass in overtime, then snapping a wrist shot past startled Boston netminder Sugar Jim Henry. *HNIC*'s cameras caught the ensuing bedlam: Richard raced and found Lach, embracing him with crashing force. The two tumbled to the ice where Richard, beyond excited, continued to hug his teammate. The Forum celebrated Montreal's first Cup in seven years with a continuous roar that reached a climax when Richard was awarded an assist. (An instantaneous bit of universally accepted historical revisionism — Maurice never touched the puck.) Through it all, Lach wore a look of dazed joy. Later, we discovered the Rocket broke Elmer's nose during their mid-air bear hug.

Happy Daze are here again. Elmer Lach salutes the Forum crowd moments after scoring the overtime Cup-winner. Rocket Richard is to his left. Coach Dick Irvin, Sr., (right) has doffed his fedora to bathe in the limelight.

THE BIG FELLA'S GREATEST PLAYOFF · April 14, 1955

The Leafs' and Canadiens' annual dance partner in the spring playoffs from 1949–56 was the great Detroit team featuring the Production Line — Gordie Howe, Sid Abel and Ted Lindsay — along with goalie Terry Sawchuk and defenceman Red Kelly. Usually, the Wings took the measure of Canadian rivals. Detroit finished first every season in the years mentioned, outscoring (for instance) the Leafs by a margin of 339 goals along the way. They were almost as good in the playoffs, winning four Stanley Cups.

It was often said you couldn't appreciate Gordie Howe without a post-game scoring summary. Regular HNIC viewers of the era, however, developed a thorough appreciation of Howe's skills, marvelling in the economy of movement it took the "Big Fella" to stir from a gliding canter to full speed. Not to mention his indomitable presence in corners and the front of the net. (Defencemen moaned that it was easier to push a stalled car uphill than to move big Gordie from the slot.)

In the spring of 1955, mop-haired Howe was at his best, leading playoff scorers with nine goals and 11 assists in a sweep of the Leafs and a hellish seven-game finals victory over the Rocket-less Canadiens. With youngsters Glenn Hall, Johnny Bucyk and Norm Ullman ready to join the team, *Hockey News* suggested the Wings "were plotting to imprison the Stanley Cup forever."

But GM Jack Adams would trade Sawchuk, then Lindsay over the next two seasons, effectively ending one of hockey's great dynasties.

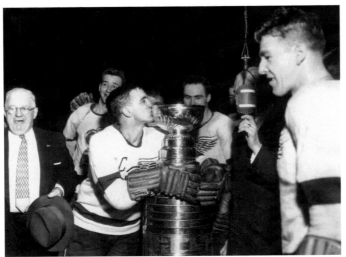

Above: Gordie Howe accepts congratulations from new "Production Line" centre "Dutch" Reibel. Below: Red Wing captain Ted Lindsay lays a kiss on the Stanley Cup. Foreground: Marcel Pronovost. Behind Lindsay, left-right: Jack Adams, unidentified player and Red Kelly.

THE RICHARD RIOT March 17, 1955

An irate fan struggles past security to confront Clarence Campbell.

For Rocket Richard and his most ardent fans, hockey was glory or humiliation. When a Montreal bus driver received news the Rocket had been suspended for the remainder of the season in the final week of the 1954–55 NHL season — with Richard on the verge of winning his first scoring title — the worker was so distraught he drove his vehicle through a flashing railroad crossing, nearly killing everyone on board.

Richard earned the suspension by slugging an official for the second time that season. In a game earlier that week in Boston, he had been clipped by Bruin Hal Laycoe. Feeling blood on his scalp, the Rocket exploded, twice breaking free from linesman Cliff Thompson to thrash his attacker. The third time that the official grabbed Richard, the Rocket dropped him like a plank.

Canadiens management pleaded Richard couldn't be held responsible for the final attack because at that point he was a bucking, blood-blinded bull. NHL President Clarence Campbell evidently disagreed. And Richard's suspension sent Montreal into an ugly sulk. Mayor Jean Drapeau publicly condemned Campbell. Radio stations fulminated against what listeners called a cruel injustice.

Crank calls to the NHL's Montreal head office the day of the riots — St. Patrick's Day — presaged what was to come. "Tell Campbell I'm an undertaker and he's going to need me in a few days," was a typical sentiment. Many women simply cried into the phone.

At the Forum, gangs began to congregate mid-afternoon, carrying signs that read *"Vive Richard"* and *"à bas Campbell."* By 8:30 game time, more than six hundred angry protesters had gathered. Many chanted, "Kill Campbell." As seen on HNIC, the game was incidental to what quickly became a public riot. With a distressed Richard watching from a goal judge's booth, Detroit made easy work of the lifeless Canadiens, jumping to a 4–1 first-period lead.

But the most pertinent action this night was in the stands. Arriving late, inadvertently inviting scrutiny, President Campbell became the target of verbal, then physical, abuse. Rotten fruit, eggs and pig's knuckles came flying his way. He pretended not to care and watched the game, making notes about the work of the referees on a pad, as was his custom.

In the first intermission, a youth sprang toward Campbell, crushing two tomatoes on his chest. Campbell rose, and pointed out his assailant. But no police came to his aid. The mob pressed in. And then, as if on cue, a tear-gas bomb went off nearby. Suddenly everyone in the crowd, including Campbell's tormentors, scrambled to the exits for safety.

A Montreal chief of detectives would later tell *Maclean's*, "The bomb-thrower protected Campbell's life by releasing it at precisely the right moment."

After that, the game was called, with Detroit winning by forfeit. But just as the Rocket could not be contained by officials earlier that week in Boston, the crowd gathered around the Forum would not be tamed by police. Cabbies were hauled out of taxis and beaten. Stores were ransacked. Windows smashed. Fires set. By the next morning, rivers of broken glass extended for miles in every direction from the Forum.

Like all great champions, the '50s Red Wings carried themselves with a certain swagger. Ted Lindsay and Gordie Howe received death threats from Toronto fans during Detroit's 1956 playoff series with the Leafs. Lindsay retaliated by scoring both the game-tying and overtime winning goals the following game in Toronto. Afterward, "Terrible Teddy" was seized by a mischievous impulse. "Going off the ice," he later told *Hockey Digest*, "I decided to put my stick with the blade up under my arm as if to pretend it was a rifle. I skated around … and kept chattering, 'rat-ta-ta-tat!'"

"Terrible" Ted Lindsay takes aim at his critics after his Red Wings defeat the Leafs in the 1956 playoffs.

LE GROS BILL April 10, 1956

Jean Beliveau picked up his early nickname, "Le Gros Bill" from the Quebec folk song "Le Voilà le Gros Bill." Here he goes one on four with the Detroit Red Wings (left-right: Tony Leswick, Marty Pavelich, Red Kelly and Terry Sawchuk).

Who was the greatest player in the '50s — the Rocket or Gordie Howe? Anyone who spent Saturday nights watching HNIC in the middle and late years of this decade suggests that the answer to that age-old question might be Jean Beliveau.

An idol in Quebec City in the early '50s, Jean Beliveau reluctantly left his native city for tantalizing trial exhibitions with the Canadiens. Turning pro with the Canadiens finally in the 1953–54 campaign, *Le Gros Bill* became a star one season later, and outscored (223 to 204) and outpointed (469 to 458) Howe through the remainder of the decade.

Certainly, Beliveau was the most exciting player during this period — an elegant, powerful skater who used his anaconda wingspan to move around hapless defencemen and goalies. In the Canadiens' successful playoff finals against Detroit in the spring of 1956, he seemed like a big kid playing with small boys, scoring seven goals in five games.

With Beliveau leading the way, the Habs would continue to win Stanley Cups — a record five in a row — right through the fifties.

PERPETUAL SCORING

March 16, 1957

Leaf youngster Dick Duff (17) fires one of 14 pucks past Gump Worsley.

"Fans haven't had this much opportunity to cheer all season," commented Foster Hewitt early in the third period of this late season game. The Rangers had clinched a playoff berth the night before, celebrating with a party that knew no curfew. They landed in Toronto with stiff hangovers and rubber legs. It was 2–0 after one period and 8–0 after two for the out-of-the-playoffs' Leafs, as coach Howie Meeker gave youngsters Bob Pulford, Dick Duff and Bob Baun lots of productive ice time. (Two games later, Frank Mahovlich made his Leaf debut, wearing number 26.) The contest also marked Teeder Kennedy's last Gardens appearance, and an appreciative crowd cheered his every point. The rout continued in the third, as Leafs scored six more times. The nicest goal of the night was a rink-long solo dash by coltish Duff (wearing number 17). "It's just perpetual motion," chirped Foster, commenting on the HNIC record 14-goal skate. Ranger goalie Gump Worsley, slim as a kitten at this point in his career, but characteristically droll, would tell Leaf counterpart Ed Chadwick after the game, "Geez, you'd think more of the shots would've just hit me." A few years later, Ward Cornell asked Worsley which team gave him most trouble? "The Rangers," he replied.

THE RUSSIANS ARE COMING November 22, 1957

Foster Hewitt is tickled to be with Thom Benson, then head of CBC-TV specials, and hockey star Sid Smith. The former Leaf (who is still wearing his old socks) played with the Whitby Dunlops against the Russians in 1957.

The Super Series in 1972 wasn't the first time Harry Sinden and Foster Hewitt were involved in a major televised game against the Big Red Machine.

In late 1957, the Soviets — with the Cold War at its most frigid — took on the Whitby Dunlops in a historic Friday-night broadcast of HNIC.

The enigmatic Russians kept two hundred sportswriters and scouts humming the day before with an (by Canadian standards) unorthodox practice. Some players sported toques. As in soccer, goalies wore different coloured jerseys. And the team was in constant, finely choreographed motion.

"They started by giving each player a puck," the *Toronto Telegram* reported. "Coach Anatoli Tarasov ordered them to go from one end to the other on one skate. While the goalie jumped four feet in the air … and [performed] other forms of weird exercises, the rest of the team skated back on one leg, shaking their wrists."

They came out the next night smokin', frightening the life out of a packed Maple Leaf Gardens by scoring two quick goals. The Whitby Dunlops — "Go, Dunnies, Go!" — scrambled furiously back, scoring in bunches and thumping every Russian in sight. (Some thumps were provided by Whitby's Harry Sinden.) All this in the first period.

Foster was hooked. "This is one of the best hockey games we've seen here in a while," Hewitt enthused when HNIC finally came on air early in the second period, with the Allan Cup champs

leading 5–2. The action was frantic for the remainder of the frame. But not as intense as the second intermission, when host Scott Young (Neil's dad) learned the Russian players he was to interview went straight to the dressing room (for a dressing down). In their place was an unsmiling colonel with a suitably grim interpreter.

Whitby forward Charlie Burns (later to play on five NHL clubs) scores one of seven goals against the Russians. Sign of things to come: Foster Hewitt referred to Whitby as "Canada" throughout the game.

"Why do some Soviet players wear toques?" Young innocently inquired. "This is not so very important," was the chill response.

The Whitby team eventually won 7–2 and would go on to defeat many of these Soviet players, toques and all, for the gold medal in the 1958 World Championships.

Bill at the mike. Foster Hewitt's son made his HNIC debut at the age of eight, in 1936.

The HNIC season started with a surprise this night when the game snapped on with the image of Leaf defenceman Steve Kraftcheck on the ice, shaking off an injury. After welcoming viewers and giving the score, Foster Hewitt announced, "This season, play-by-play for radio and TV, I'm very proud to say, will be handled by my son, Bill Hewitt. After 30 years of play-by-play, my efforts will be interjecting highlights and comments during the course of play."

With that, Bill Hewitt took over from his dad for a smooth-as-Max-Bentley 23-year run. For if Foster Hewitt proved a hard act to follow — especially with the living legend looming over his protégé's shoulder at first — Bill never showed the strain on air.

The younger Hewitt's presence gave Leaf broadcasts a reassuringly familiar feel, for Bill sounded exactly like Foster back in the '30s. Like his father, Bill Hewitt was also lifted by great hockey. And perhaps the secret reason we look back on the great Leaf-Canadien rivalry from the '60s as full of such deliciously tense affairs is because the games were being translated for us by master dramatists, Danny Gallivan and Bill Hewitt.

Hewitt never craved the attention that came with his position. And colleagues sometimes got the sense he was a reluctant heir to the Hewitt microphone. (Beginning at the age of eight, in 1936, Bill broadcast a few minutes of a Leaf game in what was called "Young Canada Night.")

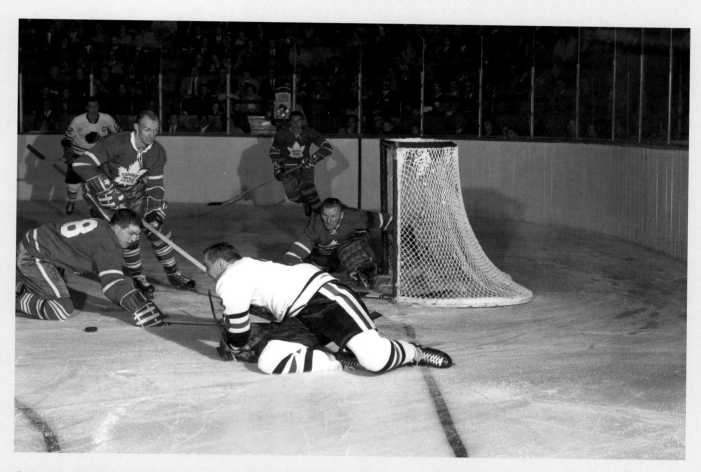

Action from Bill Hewitt's first telecast. Johnny Bower, in his Maple Leaf debut, is poised to perform one of his patented poke checks. Sliding in front, Toronto rookie Carl Brewer (18) and Chicago's Danny Lewicki. In the far background, behind Leaf defenceman Steve Kraftcheck, you can see the *HNIC* corner goal camera that was used from 1957 through to 1959.

Bill once explained his decision to retire, after an illness in 1981, by saying, "Dad had just decided to retire himself and I recalled making a pact with him when I was 16 that I would retire when he did. So I kept my word."

But it could never be said that Bill's passion for hockey was simulated. While in retirement at a 100-acre farm in Sunderland, Ontario, Hewitt regularly watched hockey on a 55-inch satellite TV. Sometimes, he once told a reporter, he turned off the sound and broadcast the games himself. The great thing, he said, was that if the game ceased to interest him, he could always go away and do something else.

A BOY AT THE LEAFS' CAMP

March 7, 1959

The kid who almost killed the Leafs, Don Keenan shakes hands with Johnny Bower after the post-game, three-star skate.

It was a story that might have served as the basis for one of Scott Young's stirring juvenile hockey dramas — *Scrubs on Skates* or *A Boy at the Leafs' Camp*. With Toronto struggling to make the playoffs, Boston Bruins arrived in town with a sick goalie (Harry Lumley: food poisoning). Lynn Patrick and Milt Schmidt, the Bruin GM and coach, sought out Leaf counterpart Punch Imlach just before the game, asking for news on the Leafs "house goalie."

"Where's Keenan?" Punch shouted into the crowd. Don Keenan, a fresh-faced 21-year-old, who later played for the University of Toronto, wandered down from the stands. "Like you to meet Milt Schmidt," Imlach said, introducing Keenan to the Boston coach. While Keenan hopped into his pads, Schmidt raced to find Imlach again. "How old is this kid?" the Bruin coach asked. "About 16," Punch guessed. "Seriously?" "Seriously," Imlach chuckled, adding, "I can only say I tried the Blind Institute but they had no one available." Punch stopped laughing once the game began. Keenan proved more than capable in the only game of his NHL career.

The score was one-all well into the third. A Boston goal could mean the Leafs were out of the playoffs. But then Ron Stewart punched two past Keenan, and Carl Brewer, just sprung from the penalty box, scored on a breakaway. Keenan, however, was named the game's third star. Imlach was still having heart palpitations after the game. "That kid almost killed us out there," he told reporters. "I told the boys to shoot more. He had to be nervous. I would have been. But he came through."

THE END OF AN AFFAIR

April 14, 1960

A rare happy photograph of NHL President Clarence Campbell and "Morris" Richard shortly before the Montreal captain accepted the team's fifth consecutive Stanley Cup.

They were so good, the NHL had to make a law against them. Before the great late '50s Montreal dynasty, teams scored as often as they could during a two-minute advantage.

But with cagey Doug Harvey at the point alongside designated shooter Boom Boom Geoffrion, and butter-smooth playmakers Jean Beliveau and Dickie Moore upfront, not to mention the always ravenous Rocket Richard prowling the slot for fat rebounds, Canadiens routinely piled up two or more goals a power play.

So the league decided to limit teams to one goal a penalty in order to encourage competition. Didn't matter. Toe Blake's team won everything in sight from 1956–60. In the spring of 1960, the Habs beat Toronto four straight to win their fifth Stanley Cup. The last two games were in Maple

Leaf Gardens and concluded a long simmering romance — an affair really — between the Rocket and Leaf fans.

In the third game, Toronto fans broke into sustained applause when Maurice scored what would be his last goal — a gesture the Rocket acknowledged during a post-game presentation of the Stanley Cup (NHL President Clarence Campbell introduced him as "Morris" Richard), when the Rocket told the crowd, "The best place to win [the Stanley Cup] is right here in Toronto."

Things weren't as rosy in the Gardens minutes afterward when HNIC's Ward Cornell, hurrying from guest to guest, identified Leaf owner Stafford Smythe as Montreal HNIC colour man, Frank Selke, Jr.

Smythe swiftly corrected him. "I'm sorry," Ward offered. "You should be," Smythe grumbled.

The Rocket's red glare is in evidence as he scores his last ever NHL goal on Leaf goalie Johnny Bower. Defending for the Leafs are Allan Stanley (26) and Tim Horton (7).

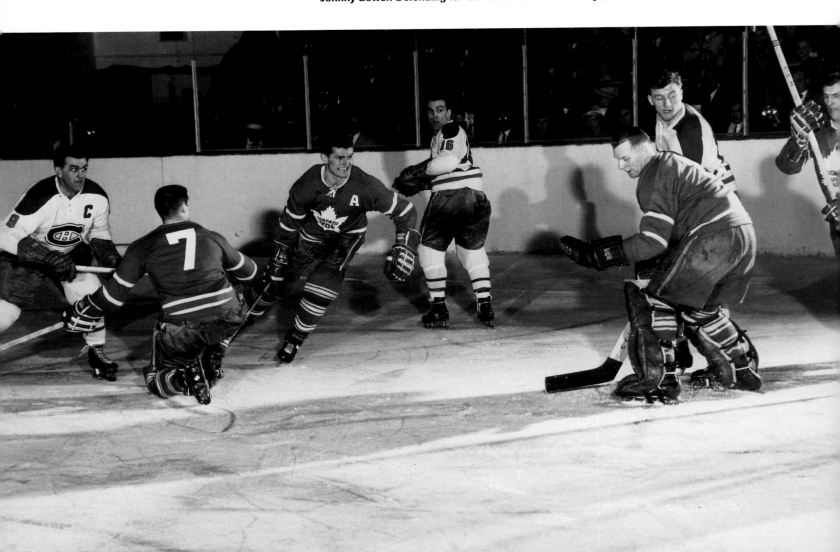

1960–61 to 1969–70

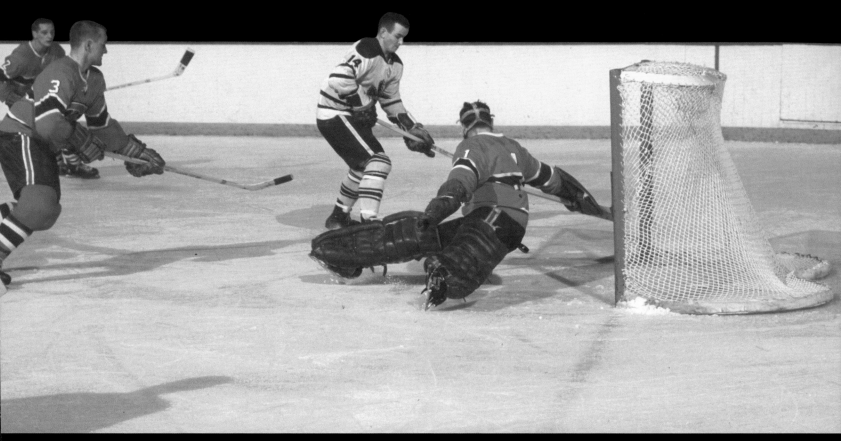

Bobby Hull, missing his two front teeth, accepts kudos from a fan shortly before Chicago wins the Stanley Cup. A pensive Eric Nesterenko (15) looks on in the foreground.

The Chicago Black Hawks hoist "Mr. Goalie," Glenn Hall, shortly after the team won its first Cup since 1938. The Chicago-Detroit series was the first all-American finals since 1950.

"That's the first one, Ward," a grinning Bobby Hull, number 16 of the Chicago Black Hawks, told HNIC's Ward Cornell minutes after his team dispatched the Red Wings to win the 1960–61 Stanley Cup.

Hull had reason to be optimistic. After leading the league in scoring in his third season, the 22-year-old went on another scoring rampage in these playoffs, leading all shooters with his eight goals.

Even though his team would never again win a championship, Hull remained a commanding hockey presence throughout the '60s. (For Hull alone, HNIC would tamper with alternating Toronto and Montreal games nationally, very often going out of sequence to accommodate a Canadian visit from the Golden Jet.)

In 1962, Hull tallied 50 goals, every goal scorer's Everest. Then came a record 54 in 1965–66, followed by an incredible 58 markers in 1968–69. Trophies and endorsements were his inevitable due. There he was in magazines, stripped to the waist, a blond Bond modelling bathing suits. On TV, he pitched hair cream, advising kid brother, Dennis, to "lay off the greasy kid's stuff."

But it was on the ice where Hull truly captured our imagination, circling the net, legs crossing over, ready to explode up the wing and unleash another fabulous slapshot.

They were a superbly co-ordinated defensive team, led by the blueline pairings of Horton and Stanley, Brewer and Baun. (HNIC's Scott Young once said that Allan Stanley "played defence like he had oncoming forwards on a string, drawn toward him.") They also had pony express Hall-of-Fame goaltenders — Bower for two games, then masked marvel Don Simmons for a week — and a mulish tendency to play just hard enough to win. Perhaps only to torment coach Punch Imlach.

These were the Leafs who blossomed every spring in the early '60s, winning the Cup in 1962–63–64. In the first win, Toronto was down 1–0 to Chicago in the third period, game six, when the Black Hawks let up, giving the master counter-punchers room to work. First, Frank Mahovlich threw a quick blind backhand to a breaking Bob Nevin for the equalizer. Minutes later, Tim Horton set up Dick Duff to win the game. Afterward, in a suddenly quiet Chicago Stadium, the Leafs performed what would be an annual tradition, as first Al Arbour, then Bobby Baun, Alan Stanley and Eddie Litzenberger crushed, flattened, trampled and squashed Punch's trademark fedora.

Four frames from 1962: Top right: Bob Nevin scores tying goal against Glenn Hall. Directly below: Dick Duff tallies winner. Third frame: jubilant Leafs gather around goalie Don Simmons. Bottom: Punch Imlach congratulates Duff. Imlach is all smiles in the picture, but a half-hour later in the dressing room, he was screaming at his charges to stop celebrating and start packing their bags for the team's return trip to Toronto.

LEAFS' HALFBACK OPTION

December 7, 1963

Carl Brewer probably never belonged in the decade he played his best hockey. He was the first NHLer with an agent (Alan Eagleson) and he wanted understanding more than instruction from his coach (Punch Imlach). He was also a born instigator who didn't like to fight. When he quit the Leafs for the Canadian national team in the mid-sixties, Brewer was handed a player form. Under nickname, he wrote down "Skitz."

On this evening, Brewer became entangled with the Hawks' Murray Balfour. Bobby Hull told the ref to let them go, and go they did, with Balfour chasing a backward-dancing Brewer for a good five minutes before grabbing and steering the Leaf toward the boards. Other fights broke out, but HNIC cameras remained on Brewer as Balfour pushed him sprawling backward into an open exit, lunging in on top of him. At this point, the combatants were swallowed up by team officials.

Suddenly, from the top of our TV frame, a blond man in a suit then flew down the stairs past security into the melee after Balfour. Brewer's protector, it was much later revealed, was Toronto Argonaut running back Dick Shatto.

Watching an old HNIC tape of the fight years later, Brewer said, "I knew my career was over" after the fight. He would quit the Leafs two seasons later, at age 26.

Top: Leafs and Hawks congregate off to the side as Carl Brewer (circled) takes on Murray Balfour. In seconds, the Chicago forward will steer Brewer to the Leafs bench. **Below:** Referee Frank Udvari angrily gestures to Hawks' Reg Fleming who had initiated the bench-clearing brawl by spearing Eddie Shack. Leafs captain George Armstrong looks on.

ELEVEN NOTHING January 18, 1964

Canadian kids twice experienced *A Hard Day's Night* in 1964. The joyous musical, starring The Beatles, hit theatres in August. Earlier that year, however, another, less salutary version came to HNIC when Boston waffled Toronto, 11–0.

Mind you, this wasn't the late sixties Bruins. Numbers four and seven were McCord and Kurtenbach. Boston was in last place. And Toronto was in the midst of a three-year championship run.

Televised games didn't begin airing until the end of the first period back then. (Who'd fork out two bucks a seat if entire

Goalie Don Simmons watches one of the few Bruin shots that didn't end up in his net in what Foster Hewitt called "a Boston tea party." Also pictured, Jerry Toppazini (21), Allan Stanley (26), and in the background, Tim Horton and Boston's Johnny Bucyk.

games were televised? teams feared.) With the delay, fans snapping on their TVs at 8:30 were giddy with anticipation. Who knew how many goals the Big M had by now?

Finally, our screens were alive with hockey. What was this? Derisive hooting. Penalty probably. Then we noticed Red Kelly (white helmet) and Frank Mahovlich skating head down. *Uh-oh.*

Next came the news that ruined this Saturday night clear through until Tuesday:

"Hello Canada and hockey fans in the United States, Bill Hewitt here at Maple Leaf Gardens. The score, Boston Bruins, *six*, Toronto Maple Leafs, *nothing.*"

"What?"

"Six nothing!" Hewitt repeated, sensing we didn't believe him the first time.

The period ended in angry boos. Cut to commercial. A rousing nautical jingle from Molson's: *"Ride to the sea in ships, my lads …"* Afterward, Bill Hewitt and analyst Bill Walker, sports editor of the *Toronto Telegram*, exchanged anguished comments. "I've never seen a Leaf team so humiliated," Walker sighed.

The Bruins laid on two more coats of shellac in the second and third periods. Old pros, the Leafs accepted the beating as random luck. A giggling Red Kelly hid his face late in the game, while Toronto fans, always noble in defeat, hollered, "We want 10! … 11! … and 12!"

Scribe Dick Beddoes ("Bed clothes" we called him) caught the mood of the game in the *Globe and Mail* the following news day: "From this day forward, January 18th, 1964, will be designated as the date when the lamb backed the butcher into a corner in Maple Leaf Gardens and carved his initials on him with a meat cleaver."

THIRD STAR KILLS CANADIENS April 9, 1964

Dave Keon could skate as fast and far as a December wind. A peerless defender who scored many key goals, Keon was "the most valuable player on the great Leaf teams we played in the sixties," according to Jean Beliveau. In the 1964 spring playoffs, Davie scored all three Leaf goals in a 3–1, seventh-game win that eliminated the hometown Canadiens from the playoffs. Still, for all his efforts, he was named third star — after goalies Johnny Bower and Charlie Hodge. Decades later he would surprise Dick Irvin by jokingly asking the HNIC Montreal colour man what a player had to do in Montreal to get first or second star?

A silky move by soon-to-score Dave Keon (14) leaves Montreal goalie Charlie Hodge up in the air and out of the way. Chasing in vain: J.C. Tremblay (3) and Jacques Laperriere (2).

THE NOVOCAINE GOAL

April 23, 1964

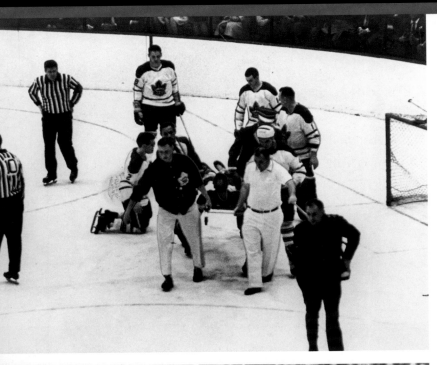

Top: Bobby Baun is carted off shortly after hearing his leg "pop." In overtime, Baun (21) sneaked onto the ice to give Toronto a game-six Stanley Cup finals win. The puck behind Red Wing goalie Terry Sawchuk was undoubtedly scored by a *Toronto Telegram* photo editor using a felt-tip pen. Celebrating Leafs include Dave Keon (14), George Armstrong (10) and Billy Harris (15).

Bob Baun only scored 40 times in his career, but every year thousands of fans remind him of the goal he scored in the 1964 Stanley Cup finals.

Baun's Leafs were down three games to two to the Red Wings, in Detroit, when Baun took a shot from Gordie Howe in the third period of a tie game. A shift later he heard something pop in his leg, and then crumpled in agony. Cameras showed him being carted off the ice, staring at his treasonous ankle.

Legend has Baun returning in overtime, but with two minutes left in regular play. HNIC colour man Keith Dancy can be heard shouting, "What a rugged performer that Baun is! My goodness, carried off on a stretcher, five minutes later, there he is on the blueline."

His ankle frozen and taped, Baun sat in the Leaf dressing room waiting for overtime, gripped with a single fear. "I was worried," he would say later, "you figure if you get hurt, someone is going to take your place."

Two minutes into overtime, Leaf coach Punch Imlach called out for "Brewer and HILLMAN." Baun leapt over the boards in Hillman's place. Seconds later, a clearing pass came to the blueline. The defenceman slapped at it, just trying to keep play in Detroit's zone. The puck fluttered toward the net, nicked defenceman Bill Gadsby's stick, and then hopped lazily over Terry Sawchuk's shoulder for the historic winning goal.

He was a hero in New York, but when Andy Bathgate came to Toronto in a late-season trade, the star winger was to his new teammates the guy who took the place of lifelong Leafs Bob Nevin and Dick Duff. It didn't help that Bathgate was a talker in a dressing room devoid of rah-rah types. Or that he didn't score much late in the season. Early in the scoreless game seven of the finals, however, number nine proved his worth, stealing the puck from Junior Langlois at the Leaf blueline, and then dashing up the right side. Once in the Detroit end, Bathgate found Terry Sawchuk in a crouch and heard a goal-scorer's mantra go off in his head: "*Short side, high, far side, low.*" Twenty feet out, he let go a perfect snapshot, placing the puck inside the crook of the goal post and crossbar. Afterward, *HNIC* cameras showed the jubilant Leafs chase their new teammate back to the bench. Andy ignored and ducked every one of them, however. He'd said what he wanted to say in scoring the winning goal of the Stanley Cup finals.

Above: Andy Bathgate scoring a goal-scorer's goal. After number nine's breakaway score, Leafs added markers from Dave Keon, Red Kelly and George Armstrong, on the way to a decisive 4–0, seventh-game Stanley Cup win.

Below: Rally round the Cup, boys. Left–right, back row: a helmeted Billy Harris, Jim Pappin (looking down) and grinning Andy Bathgate. Front row, seated: Johnny Bower, George Armstrong (10), Bob Pulford (20) and Bobby Baun (21) all admire the shine on Lord Stanley's mug.

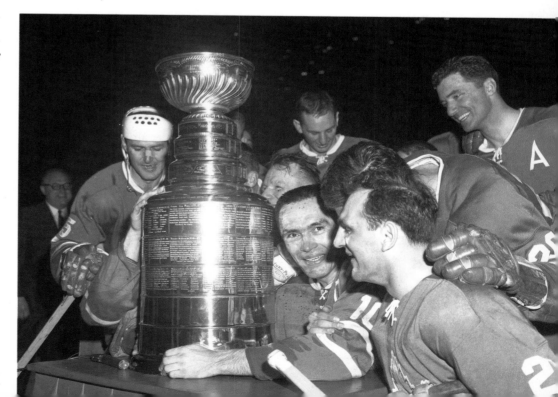

Stan Mikita and Normie Ullman (7) wait for a faceoff in Ullman's historic game.

When a team is down two with six seconds left, HNIC's Harry Neale will sometimes crack, "Unless Normie Ullman is in the building, this game's over." Knowledgeable fans chuckle, remembering that Ullman famously scored two goals in five seconds. The game in question was a Sunday night playoff match in Detroit. The score was 2–1 Chicago when Detroit's Ullman grabbed the puck at centre, crossed the blueline and snapped a softie between defenceman Matt Ravlich's legs 40 feet along the ice past a startled Glenn Hall, an accomplishment that sent the Olympia into hysterical delight. Eggs were lobbed in Hall's direction. Out came the cleaning crew. Five minutes later, the puck was dropped.

Eric Nesterenko cleared the puck onto Ullman's stick. The Detroit centre drifted in. Ravlich lunged for him, remembering number seven's last visit. Hall drifted over to protect his glove side, remembering number seven's last visit. And the puck ticked Ravlich's skate and skimmed 40 feet along the ice just past Hall on the stick side. Remarkably, neither goal was shot any harder than a shinny pass to your kid sister.

They didn't quite have the polish or élan of the 1955–60 or 1976–79 Montreal Canadiens dynasties. Stork-like Jacques Laperriere with his curious, egg-beater skating style wasn't Doug Harvey. And as sportswriter Dick Beddoes once observed, loosely packed goalie Gump Worsley resembled "a pound of butter that has been left out of the fridge overnight." Centres Beliveau, the Pocket Rocket and Backstrom were state of the art, but the wingers — except for pinball blur Yvon Cournoyer — seldom lifted fans and TV viewers from their seats in the manner of the Rocket or Guy Lafleur.

Toe Blake enjoys a Coke while rubbing overtime hero Claude Provost's noggin in the Habs' dressing room shortly after the Habs eliminated the three-time Cup champion Leafs.

Still, the mid-sixties Canadiens competed in the Stanley Cup finals every spring from 1965 until 1969 and came close to equalling a record five championships in a row.

The team's great character actors: hatchet-faced tough guy John Ferguson, "big, burly" Ted Harris, Terry Harper, and especially choppy-skating Claude Provost, got them through blood-soaked playoff wars with the Leafs during the mid-sixties. It was Provost, in fact, who ended Toronto's three-year reign by shooting a rolling puck over Johnny Bower's shoulder in a game-six overtime.

After the game, Provost, called "Joe" by teammates, was asked by HNIC's Ward Cornell how he scored the big goal. Displaying the reserve that characterized these Canadiens, Provost stared down at this skates and said, "Well, I was lucky, Ward."

THIS IS YOUR CAPTAIN SPEAKING May 1, 1965

If it can be said that all the mid-sixties Canadiens were role players, then certainly captain Jean Beliveau played the crucial part in this team's success. For he was the club's best

Jean Beliveau's Stanley Cup never runneth over. Here, the Canadien captain enjoys his sixth (of what would be 10) NHL championships. Assistant captain Jean-Guy Talbot handles the runoff. Far right, stripped-to-his-Stanfield's Claude Provost handles a post-game interview.

player — a distinction he proved in the spring of 1965, scoring eight goals in 13 games on the way to winning the NHL's first Conn Smythe Trophy for best playoff performer. He was equally good in the team's 1968–69 Cup wins. Beliveau was as great a force in the dressing room as he was on the ice, and the great centreman came to embody all that was virtuous and noble about *le bleu-blanc-rouge*. Once, after a game, an unhappy rookie Canadien threw his sweater away in disgust. Beliveau walked over and carefully lifted the jersey up off the floor. "This sweater," he said gravely, "never lands on the floor again."

DID THE POCKET ROCKET KNOCK IT IN? May 5, 1966

Before instant replay became the Supreme Court of Appeal, Henri Richard killed Detroit with one of hockey's most controversial Stanley Cup goals. The Wings shocked the Habs, winning 3–2 and 5–2 in Montreal to open these finals, courtesy of the acrobatics of netminder Roger Crozier. The little goalie was hurt in game three, however, and the series swung in Montreal's favour, with Canadiens winning three straight. Crozier returned for game six in Detroit and was again performing miracles as the contest went into overtime. That's when Henri Richard carried play into the Detroit zone, squeezing around Gary Bergman. The two fell in a tangle and were met by the sliding Crozier. Upon colliding, the twin heaps spun in opposite directions, with the object of their interest sliding into the net. Crozier jumped up, motioning. *Richard pushed it in!* Thinking quickly, coach Toe Blake instructed his team to congratulate the Pocket Rocket before officals had time to think.

John Ferguson would later suggest Henri might have nudged the puck in with his arm, although replays were inconclusive. The Wings were unhappy, in any case, because the team had now lost in the finals in 1961–63–64 and 1966. This is perhaps why Crozier won the Conn

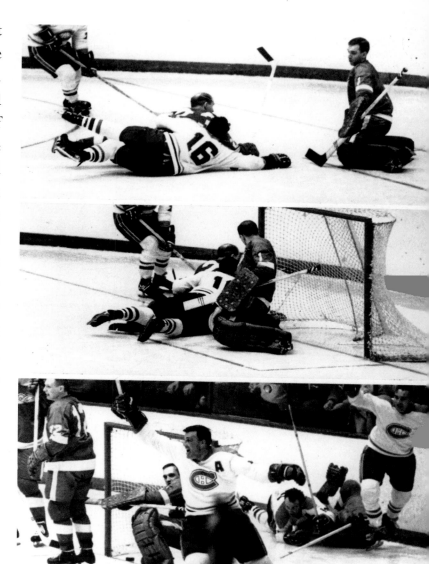

A three-sequence shot shows Henri Richard sliding in safe with the Cup-winning goal.

Smythe trophy and a car as a consolation prize, a decision that infuriated J.C. Tremblay — master of the flip shot — who had played particularly well in these playoffs. Visibly distraught after the club's Cup win — "they gave the &7@$ car to Crozier" — Tremblay was placated by team boosters a few weeks later when a banquet was held to honour the Canadiens and a car was awarded to the team's best playoff performer. J.C., of course.

WHAT IN BLUE BLAZERS?

October 22, 1966

In an effort to distinguish *HNIC* crews from orange-coated CBC sports crews, hockey TV personnel began wearing sky blue blazers in the fall of 1966, when colour came to Canadian television.

Molson's took out newspaper ads heralding the technology — "Here it comes! Hockey in colour on TV! This Saturday and throughout the year! Brought to you by the Big Ale in the Big Land." But, in truth, hockey players resisted the advance, which required brighter arena lights.

During the first colour game in Toronto, Johnny Bower claimed he got flashbulb blindness when looking up at the clock. He and defenceman Kent Douglas both wore raccoon eyeshadow. The complaints soon ceased, however. Jean Beliveau would comment, "It didn't take too long before we asked ourselves how we managed to play so long in the dark."

Maybe the biggest challenge in *HNIC*'s going to colour was left to executive director Ralph Mellanby. He had to talk Foster Hewitt, who continued to come on after the game to name the three stars, into wearing makeup and a mod blazer. Mellanby took the broadcast legend to lunch, fearing the worst, only to discover Foster was hip to *HNIC*'s new look.

Ranger Harry Howell and Toronto's Tim Horton wrestle for the puck in front of Johnny Bower in the first colour game on *HNIC*. The Leaf goalie is wearing black eyeshadow to reflect the glare of the new colour TV lights.

SATURDAY NIGHT PET

The show began with her name over the shot of a rose draped across sheet music. Then the band hit "Love and Marriage" and announcer Gil Christie purred, "Now let's meet and greet, your pet … *Ju-u-liette!*"

Between 1956 and 1966, singer Juliette Agustina Cavazzi showed up every night after *HNIC*, welcoming winding-down hockey fans with a perky shout, "Hi there, everybody."

She wasn't much of a hockey fan at first. "When I arrived in Toronto from Vancouver with my husband on St. Patrick's Day, 1954, [the show's producer] was excited because he had Leaf tickets," Juliette recalls. "'Hockey!' I said. 'I don't watch hockey.' I didn't go."

But hockey fans watched *Juliette*. Her bright cheer seemed the perfect ending for a home-team win. And maybe because the Canadiens and Leafs were always winning back then, Juliette was a long-standing Saturday night hit.

Juliette Agustina Cavazzi, or as everybody called her, "Juliette." Bobby Gimby was the show's musical director for a while. Guests included the occasional Toronto Maple Leaf (who tried to sing), Don Messer and (every Christmas) the Friendly Giant, Rusty and Jerome. Juliette's familiar sign off was always, "Good night, Mom."

DANNY BOY

Seated: Montreal's great HNIC talent, Danny Gallivan and (to his left) René Lecavalier, in their Forum broadcast booth.

Danny Gallivan was hockey's great lyricist. Two generations of *HNIC* fans sang his music on streets, schoolyards and rinks from Corner Brook to Kitimat.

Play-by-play man for *les Glorieux*, the Montreal Canadiens, from 1952 to 1984, Gallivan's impassioned delivery and ecstatic wordplay informed how we understand and talk hockey.

Playing the sport, we'd repeat favourite Gallivanisms in describing our own efforts. A quick goalie made a "larcenous save." Stalwart defenders were "burly" like Ted Harris or "truculent" in the manner of Moose Vasko.

After serving in the army, Gallivan became a radio fixture in Halifax and was discovered while in Montreal doing a game with the Junior Habs. When Montreal hired a new broadcaster, a call went out to "that chap from the Maritimes."

It's hardly surprising a producer remembered a play-by-play man from a thousand miles away. Former partner Dick Irvin marvels at how far Gallivan's voice carried.

"To get to the English broadcast booth in the old Forum you travelled past René Lecavalier in the French booth," Irvin recalls. "The thing I remember about Danny is he was so loud I don't think I ever heard René, not even when I was right behind him.

"And once you got next to Danny, well, that's when the show began. Because Danny would swing to the right if a long pass changed direction of play. Back he'd jump a few seconds later. And he'd leap out of his seat if something exciting happened."

Gallivan was so good he made his TV debut while still on radio. *HNIC* didn't begin broadcasting in English out of Montreal until the 1953–54 season. Before then, English Quebecers turned to the "French channel" while listening to Danny on radio.

GALLIVANTING

Here, for connoisseurs of the work of Danny Gallivan, is a short list of signature calls:

"Oh, and Plante kicks his pad out in rapier-like fashion!"

"Geoffrion creases the post with a cannonading drive ..."

"With Beliveau's goal the Leafs now face the Herculean task ..."

"Provost makes a visitation to the penalty box ..."

"Rousseau just failed to negotiate contact with that high pass from Laperriere."

"The Ferguson-Shack melee was a real donnybrook, if not an outright brouhaha ..."

"Crozier makes an enormous save!"

"'Where is it?' says Hull, but the puck is lost in Gump Worsley's paraphernalia ..."

"Savard avoids Clarke with a deft spinnerama move ..."

"Lafleur gobbles up the puck and away he goes ..."

"Little Henri — the Pocket Rocket — has put in 20 years of yeoman service ..."

"They bang away at it! Oh, and Dryden stymies Esposito with a scintillating save ..."

"The Boston Garden is festooned in banners ..."

"A classic Robinsonian effort has given Montreal the lead ..."

Canada and Terry Sawchuk both enjoyed a centennial in 1967. The same spring Canada celebrated its 100th anniversary, Sawchuk recorded his milestone 100th shutout against Bobby Hull and the Chicago Black Hawks. Here Terry awaits an interview in HNIC studios. (A month later, when the playoffs began, the traditional Maple Leaf crest would be replaced by the symbol from the Canadian flag — a gesture that marked the Toronto club's salute to Expo year.)

The many moods of Terry Sawchuk. Above: the great goalie appears downcast prior to a post-game interview marking his 100th shutout. (You can see Ward Cornell's head over a crew member's shoulder.) Below: Terry is all smiles for a cameraman prior to the same HNIC visit.

HABS BOOT RANGERS

April 6, 1967

All great Canadien teams were capable of spontaneous combustion. Firewagon hockey, it was called, and the Habs could turn the sirens on seemingly at will. In the first game of the 1967 semis against New York, the Rangers carefully built a 4–1 lead with 10 minutes to play. A raw anger gripped the Forum. Then Claude Provost beat Eddie Giacomin from an impossible angle. The goal "was like a blazing torch thrown into an open case of fireworks," according to *HNIC* analyst Red Fisher. The first noise came from the Forum crowd — an untamed animal roar. J.C. Tremblay scored within seconds and down came enough rubber boots to fill a department store. Even though the Rangers were still up one, the game was all over. "When those galoshes came down in the Forum, the other team was dead," remembers defenceman Terry Harper. "Some nights, you'd look out there and the galoshes were so thick they looked like leaves under a tree in the fall … I never saw a team come back after those galoshes come pouring down."

Sure enough, Ferguson, Backstrom and Beliveau fired in three more goals, concluding an astonishing 6–4 Montreal comeback.

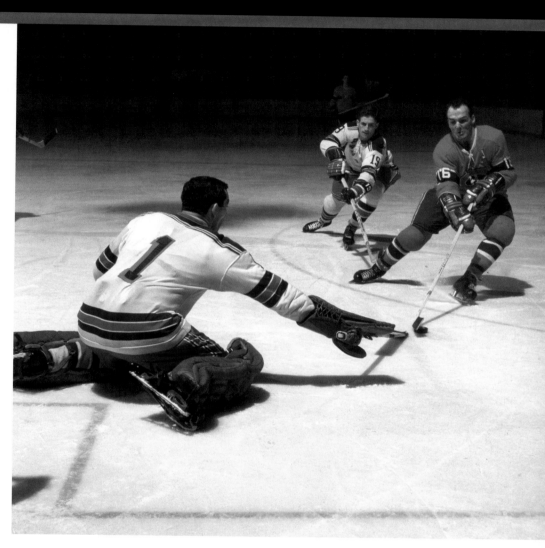

Dipping, darting Henri Richard escapes checker Jean Ratelle (19) to move in on Ed Giacomin.

TAKING THE WIND OUT OF WINDY CITY April 15, 1967

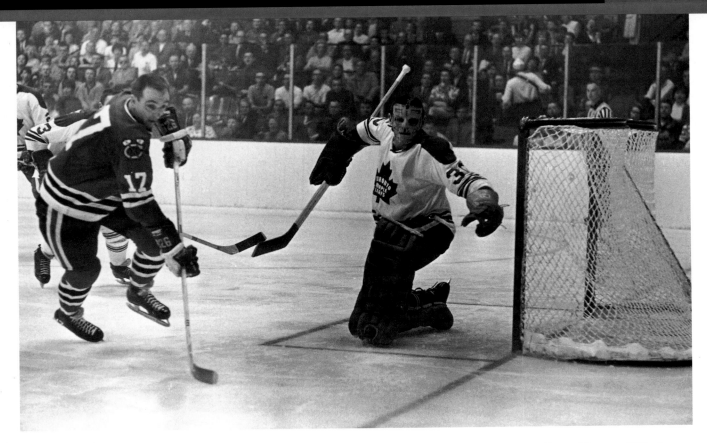

It was, many believe, the best demonstration of goaltending ever. With the Leafs-Hawks playoffs tied at two games (and goals) apiece, Terry Sawchuk replaced Johnny Bower in the Toronto net to begin the second period, game five. The era's best shooters — Bobby Hull, Stan Mikita, Phil Esposito and Kenny

The whippet, Kenny Wharram (17), chases a Terry Sawchuk rebound into the corner. Many in the crowd are wearing shirts. The playoff game was held on an unseasonably warm spring afternoon. By the third period, the Chicago arena was hotter than July.

Wharram — combined for 37 shots in 40 minutes. The most memorable came from Hull's curved blade — a rising, 30-foot missile that caught Terry under his shoulder pad, sending him flopping lifelessly to the ice. Somehow he got up, however, and, playing on guile and muscle memory, he turned back more than a dozen certain goals, leading Toronto to a 4—2 win. In the dressing room afterward, it took the 37-year-old goalie an eternity to change. When he finally took off his undershirt, he provided teammates with vivid proof of an afternoon's valour. "Goalies back then didn't have near the protection they do today," remembers teammate Ron Ellis. "Terry had ugly blue bruises all up and down his arms and shoulders. One shoulder was swollen and he could hardly move. It looked like he'd been badly beaten in a fight."

The end of the six-team era was punctuated by the last Stanley Cup playoff finals involving long-time rivals Montreal and Toronto. The series defined for us all what was great about the two teams that won nine of 10 Stanley Cups in the sixties. By game six, in Toronto, the Canadiens had outplayed the Leafs in three games, but only won two. (Bower stole game three for the Leafs in overtime.) The Leafs needed one more win. The final game was so "tense you could've grated carrots on fans' goosebumps," in the immortal words of sportswriter Dick Beddoes. With the Leafs up 2–1, there was a faceoff in Toronto's end. Coach Imlach threw out his veterans — Horton, Stanley, Armstrong, Pulford, Kelly. Having pulled his goalie, Toe Blake countered with six skaters led by Beliveau. Referee John Ashley dropped the puck. HNIC's Bill Hewitt told us what happened next:

> All set for the faceoff now. Fifty-five seconds left. Armstrong goes over to the boards. And it's electrifying here at Maple Leaf Gardens at the moment. Here we go for the faceoff … Stanley talking to Kelly. The puck is dropped. Kelly up to Pulford. Pulford gets it up to Armstrong. Armstrong waits. He shoots. *He scores!*

Above top: Ralph Backstrom (6) and Marcel Pronovost await a shot from the blueline in front of Terry Sawchuk. Below: sedate Leaf veterans collect their fourth Stanley Cup in six years. Left-right: Bob Pulford, Jim Pappin, Johnny Bower, Pete Stemkowski, Larry Hillman. Milan Marcetta, George Armstrong kneeling with the Cup, Larry Jeffrey (in suit), Marcel Pronovost, and Mike Walton.

BETWEEN TWO SOLITUDES

Dick Irvin was a hockey broadcast renaissance man, working over the course of his long tenure at *HNIC* as host, colour man and play-by-play commentator.

In each of these roles, the broadcaster assumed whatever demeanour the job required. Working with flamboyant Danny Gallivan, Irvin was an expert counter-puncher, getting in short, sharp observations when Gallivan paused for breath. But when paired with the sometimes taciturn Scotty Bowman, Irvin grew more personable — became more of a storyteller.

Being Montreal-based, Irvin had to withstand occasional criticisms that he was a homer — a charge that all *HNIC* on-air personnel inevitably face. In his book *Now Back to You Dick*, Irvin tells the story of the day he snapped back at a TV critic.

Irvin was in Edmonton attending a private function when a friend who worked at Imperial Oil showed him a letter from an irate fan. The man was returning his gas credit card to protest Irvin's work in a 7–2 Montreal win over Toronto. Another guest knew the complainant. Irvin asked for his number and was soon on the phone:

"This is Dick Irvin of *Hockey Night in Canada*."

"Uh, oh yes."

"I understand you wrote a letter to Imperial Oil because you were upset with my work."

"Yes, that's right. … I'm just such a Maple Leaf fan I couldn't stand to listen to you that night. You drove me up the wall."

Just as Irvin suspected. "Sir, you know I'm the colour commentator and my job is to describe replays after each goal."

"Yes, I know."

"Let's see. Canadiens scored seven goals and each one was replayed twice. That means you had to watch the puck go into your team's net about 21 times. Was that my fault?"

The voice on the other end of the line suddenly became very small. "No."

DANNY AND DICK

When I first appeared on HNIC in 1966–67, the last season of the original six teams, I had no idea I would be still working on the show 38 seasons later, when the NHL consisted of 30 teams.

It has been a great run — great players, great moments and great games. But, looking back, the best memories inevitably involve people I've worked with — the men and women of HNIC who, year after year, on and off camera, do such wonderful work in producing Canada's number one television program.

I have to begin, of course, with Danny Gallivan. When Danny was in the booth, young broadcasters of that era would have given a lot to work 17 games with a legend like him. I was lucky to work beside him in the booth for 17 years. During that time, we never rehearsed or even met before a game to discuss the upcoming broadcast. Danny hated meetings, which caused a tense moment or two with the producer. But he was the constant professional, always at the top of his game.

Hockey broadcasting pioneers like Danny Gallivan and Foster Hewitt made an impression on the viewing public that continues to this day, and to a lesser degree so did the pairing of Danny and Dick.

Danny did his last broadcast in 1984, yet I still run into people who call me Danny or who ask, "Can I have your autograph, Mr. Gallivan?" I'm always flattered.

I was the first, or one of the first, HNIC announcers to interview future broadcasting stars, such as Howie Meeker, Don Cherry and Harry Neale, when they began their careers on the show.

I sat beside Bob Cole, Chris Cuthbert, Greg Millen, John Davidson and numerous others when they first joined the show in the broadcast booth.

Great guys. Great broadcasters. Like I say, my best moments are the people of HNIC and I'm proud to be one of them.   *Dick Irvin, Jr.*

DOLLARS TO DONUTS

October 30, 1968

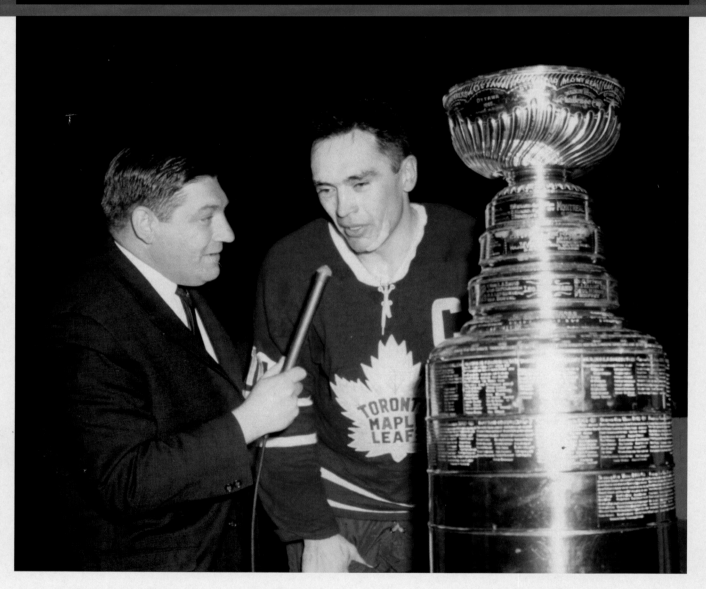

Ward Cornell chats with Leaf captain George Armstrong with what looks like a bazooka missile after the Stanley Cup presentation in 1963. The session marked the first time HNIC personnel went onto the ice to conduct post-game Stanley Cup interviews.

HNIC's first Toronto intermission host, Ward Cornell (1959–72), had the challenge of getting the first TV generation of hockey stars over stage jitters.

Given the grandeur of the stage — Foster's Hewitt's hallowed Maple Leaf Gardens — the jitters could often be charted on a Richter scale.

One time, Boston tough-guy Ted Green showed up drowning in flop sweat. Sizing up the situation during a commercial,

Ward shouted, "Cord Warnell here with Chicken Little, head of Basher's Inc." Then he turned to Green, "Chicken?"

Green stared back, petrified. "It's OK, we're not on air," Ward laughed. Green howled and a relaxed interview followed.

Another exchange that typified Ward Cornell's easy rapport with players occurred when he and Tim Horton found them-selves talking donuts one Saturday night.

Asked about retirement, 38-year-old Horton acknowledged, "Things are quite hectic these days trying to combine business with hockey."

"You're talking about your new donut chain," Cornell offered.

"Yes, Tim Horton Donuts, Ward. It's nice of you to let me get a word in about it. If I may…"

"No," Cornell said, smiling.

"Well, heck, I'm going to anyway. I'd like to say thanks to all you nice people in Hamilton and Burlington…"

"Oh, come on now," the host groaned. After Tim finished thanking his remaining customers, city by city, Ward jokingly handed him the bill for his promo spot. "And we'd like to thank you for paying to be on *Hockey Night in Canada*," he said.

"Oh, come on now," Ward Cornell groans as Hall of Fame defenceman Tim Horton makes a pitch for his then new donut chain.

He was six feet tall, but Frank Mahovlich became bigger — became the Big M! — when he found himself with the puck and the promise of open ice. Then he was off, chest high, arms swinging violently from side to side, taking ever-lengthening strides. He was the Leafs great star of the era — too bright and not constant enough for Coach Imlach. So he was traded. And when the prodigal returned as a Red Wing on this night, he announced his great talent almost immediately, grabbing a loose puck at centre, and then flying past a helpless defender before moving in on Elvis-sideburned Bruce Gamble. With a shiver of the head, he transferred rapidly from forehand to back-hand, losing Gamble in the process, and threw the puck into an empty net.

The Big M breaks in on Bruce Gamble while former linemate Dave Keon (14) looks for a rebound.

THE MIGHTY QUINN April 2, 1969

Even when he played for, rather than coached, the Leafs, Pat Quinn had the billowing look of a St. Paddy's Day float. In the playoffs of his rookie year, the Toronto blue-line cop had just about enough of the Orr-Esposito Bruins, who skated circles around the Leafs in piling up a 7–0 lead. Seeing Bobby Orr swing behind his own net to ward off Brit Selby, Quinn snowshoed in and caught Orr with his head down. The superstar was out as soon as his head hit the ice. After that, the game got ugly. First, Orr's teammates, and then Boston fans had at Quinn. (He was finally taken from the penalty box as a security precaution.) Despite a third-period kamikaze attack on the entire Boston team by Leafs' Forbes Kennedy, the Bruins won this one 10–0.

Game footage of Leaf defenceman Pat Quinn "snowshoeing in" from the blueline to rub out Bruin star Bobby Orr. As always, Phil Esposito (7) is waiting for a pass. Orr (below) was out cold for several minutes.

ORRBIT May 10, 1970

Man can't fly, but the accompanying photograph proves Bobby Orr defied gravity.

Bobby Orr a split second after bringing the Stanley Cup to Boston for the first time since 1941.

When he came to our TV screens, in the autumn of 1966, the great defenceman looked more like a grocery-store bag boy than the corner cop who "manned" the National Hockey League bluelines. But even then his play defied reality. Before the 18-year-old arrived in Boston, defencemen had few prescribed chores: Stay back. Play the man. Bang the puck up the boards.

Orr changed the logic and rhythm of hockey. He could be two places at once. Leading the league in scoring at one end. Winning the best defenceman award at the other. Other players had positions. Orr played the entire rink, which seemed to tilt helpfully downward when he took off on thrilling slalom runs.

On this, his most famous goal, in the spring of 1970, Boston's number four finally acknowledged his superhero status, celebrating an overtime Stanley Cup-winning marker by flying through wild air, arms outstretched, proclaiming victory.

PIONEER NIGHTS

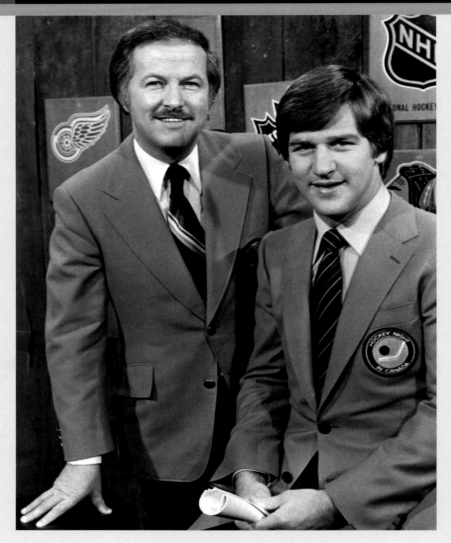

Brian McFarlane and HNIC rookie analyst Bobby Orr.

When I joined HNIC as a colour commentator in the early 1960s, beginning a 25-year association with the show, the NHL was a six-team league. Across Canada, Saturday night was reserved for hockey. And the HNIC theme song was as familiar to most of us as the national anthem.

I was fortunate enough to begin my career high in the famous gondola at Maple Leaf Gardens, with legendary play-by-play men Foster and Bill Hewitt. Colour TV was still in the future back then. Each club carried just one goalie on its roster, which meant the seventh-best goalie in the world played in the minors.

Teams played each other 14 times per season and competition was fierce, particularly between ancient rivals, Montreal and Toronto. Future Hall-of-Famers were all over the ice when these clubs met: Beliveau, the Richards, Harvey, Plante, Geoffrion and other brilliant Habs versus Bower, Horton, Stanley, Armstrong, Keon, Kelly and similarly gifted Leafs.

There were no helmets. No names on the jerseys. No player agents. No million-dollar salaries. No thought of bringing players over from Europe or scouting and recruiting college players. Certainly no talk of expansion to distant cities. Not even Vancouver.

Saturday night was hockey night. It was a tradition that began in radio in the thirties. Then, from 1952 on, families gathered in their living rooms to *watch* the game. Not that everyone made it through all three periods. Youngsters were seldom allowed to watch a complete game before being ordered off to bed.

Many of my telecast teammates — Foster and Bill, Jack Dennett, Ward Cornell and Danny Gallivan — were household names. Foster's three-star selections were as eagerly awaited as the national news and he was often accused of picking "the two goalies and Keon" far too often.

Some viewers thought Murray Westgate, who pitched commercials for Imperial Oil while wearing a cap and an Esso patch on his uniform, actually owned a service station.

We didn't know it, of course, but we were pioneers back then. And if we thought ourselves to be the luckiest broadcasters in the world, it's because we were fortunate enough to have played a part in bringing the greatest sport in the world into homes all across Canada. *Brian McFarlane*

Best Wishes Peter Puck

PUCKISH ADVENTURES

Peter Puck, a talking puck created by the legendary Hollywood animation company Hanna Barbera, was dropped into NBC hockey telecasts in 1973. He also made frequent appearances on *HNIC*. The "irrepressible imp of the ice" explained hockey's nuances to shinny newcomers without going offside with old-time viewers. Some Canadians admitted they learned from the professor of puck. Peter received thousands of letters and had his own fan club. One young viewer asked, "Does it hurt when the players hit you on your bottom?" Another wanted to marry Peter.

JUMPIN' JEHOSHAPHAT

Howie Meeker was in Montreal on business in 1968 when he bumped into broadcaster Ted Darling. After an exchange of pleasantries, Darling asked Meeker if he would be guest analyst in an upcoming Montreal-Toronto game.

K-bam! Howie Meeker lights a surprise gift from HNIC crew members: an exploding cigar. You can be sure the first words out of Howie's mouth after the burning stogie were stronger than his customary, on-air cry, "Gee Whiz!"

The 1947 NHL rookie of the year thought hockey fell through the ice in the fifties. Here was his chance to speak out on the game he loved. Only thing he had to remember was not to break into the first language of hockey — swearing — if and when he got wound up.

No one remembers Meeker's first on-air sermon, but it probably went something like: "Look at Bell-ee-voe coming in alone! Jumpin' Jehoshaphat, what's Walton doing? Looking in the stands for pretty girls? Back it up. Stop right there. Bee-u-tee-full move past Gamble and hey-hey, the big fellow puts it home, easy as picking strawberries."

"Howie was an immediate sensation," remembers HNIC executive producer Ralph Mellanby. "He changed us into real sports reporters. Howie came from Newfoundland. He didn't owe the league anything. If Beliveau had a bad game, he said it. ... No one broadcaster ever changed TV hockey coverage more than Howie."

For one thing, Meeker changed the pay scale for analysts. Until Howie, guests received $50 a visit. "No goddamn way I'm coming back from Newfoundland for [$50]," Meeker shouted when he was informed HNIC wanted him to do regular commentary. And with that, analysts began making $100 an appearance.

A CUTTING WIT

HNIC host Dave Hodge finally meets his hair-grooming match, Pittsburgh defenceman Dave Burrows.

Dave Hodge was 26 — with a stint as the Buffalo Sabres play-by-play man and a Chatham, Ontario, newspaper and radio career behind him — when, in 1971, *HNIC* executive producer Ralph Mellanby pronounced him "our new Ward Cornell."

Scrupulously well informed, with a wit as sharp as a Tacks skate, Hodge developed into a superb intermission host. Occasionally, his between-period or post-game interviews were as eventful as the game themselves.

In the eighties, Hodge developed an on-air sparring routine with Minnesota North Star forward Willie Plett. Aiming to get back at Hodge for a previous session, Plett showed up for an on-air interview with a pair of scissors, and cut off Hodge's tie. At this point, the host reached for a glass of water to collect himself, and then turned to Plett, a cumbersome skater, and said, "Geez, Willie, I didn't know you could cut to your right."

Big-time professional hockey found its way back to the West Coast when the green-blue Canucks arrived at Vancouver's Pacific Coliseum in the fall of 1970. First season, Saturday contests began at five o'clock so all HNIC games would be played in concert. Cyclone Taylor, star of the 1915 Stanley Cup-winning Vancouver Millionaires, blew into town to drop the first puck. Alas, the inaugural Canucks would boast no players of Cyclone's meteorological stature. Rookie Dale Tallon (consolation prize after Gilbert Perreault in the '70 draft) became Vancouver's first star, although stern, hardworking centre Orland Kurtenbach was arguably team MVP. Pat Quinn and Gary Doak protected little Charlie Hodge in net. The team was a TV hit right from the start though, with the Babe Pratt-Bill Good-Jim Robson broadcast team fitting in nicely on left wing next to Toronto and Montreal HNIC crews. That Vancouver shows were so good right from the start raised more than a few Central-Canadian eyebrows. "I had a friend from Ottawa, a CBC friend," remembered Vancouver producer Gord Glenn. "He saw the first game and was amazed. He thought because it wasn't Toronto or Montreal, we'd be going to black every few seconds and cameras would be falling apart."

Footage of the first ever *HNIC* game from Vancouver. Top frame: Cyclone Taylor on his way to centre ice to drop the first puck. Below: broadcasters Babe Pratt and (holding the mike) Bill Good in front of the team's first logo — a falling stick. Bottom frames: Barry Wilkins scores the first goal in Canucks history and is congratulated by Andre Boudrias and Dale Tallon.

HABS SHOCK NAPPING BRUINS April 8, 1971

The Orr-Esposito Bruins were supposed to win the Stanley Cup in 1971. They'd won the season before and handled Montreal 3–1 in the first game of the playoffs.

In game two, Boston skated all over and around Montreal during the first two periods, jumping to a 5–1 lead. Boston fans barely noticed when Henri Richard scored late in the second, figuring — *So what? Espo'd probably throw a couple past that rookie next period. What was his name … Dry-dock?*

Beliveau scored early in the third to make it a game,

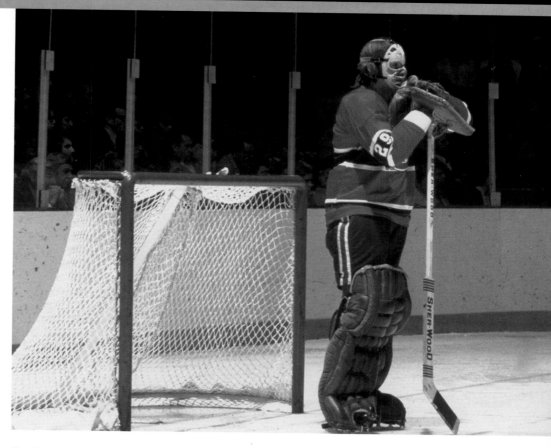

Ken Dryden in what would become a characteristic pose during his rookie playoff run.

but here came Orr with a rink-long slalom. *He shoots, he …* Oh, Dryden, that was his name, made the save. Beliveau, who saw the calendar blow off a dozen years this night, scored again. Then Lemaire tallied. Tie game. Boston rallied. Esposito had the puck alone in front. Another Dryden save. Down at the other end, Beliveau found Ferguson alone in front for the go-ahead goal. Incredibly, the Big M, Frank Mahovlich, then scored the fifth unanswered goal this period, completing the most remarkable comeback in NHL playoff history.

Boston's Gerry Cheevers would later comment, "Letting up against the [California] Seals is not like letting up against the Habs. The Flying Frenchman go glassy-eyed when they think of their tradition and pride and all that b------; they suddenly acquire adrenaline not available to other teams."

LONG-SHOT STANLEY CUP WIN May 18, 1971

The Pocket Rocket, Henri Richard, again making playoff history, beating Tony Esposito for the Stanley Cup-winning goal.

It was a Cup the Canadiens weren't supposed to win. Not with a McGill law student (Ken Dryden) in net. Not with coach Al MacNeil squabbling with Henri Richard over playing time. And not by beating both the Orr-Phil Esposito Bruins and Hull-Mikita Black Hawks. Especially not when, in the finals, Montreal was down 2–0 midway in the seventh game to the suddenly defence-conscious Hawks. It was somehow fitting then that the long-shot Canadiens got back in the game with a shot from well past the blueline by Jacques Lemaire. ("It dipped," goalie Tony Esposito moaned afterwards.) Emboldened by Lemaire's breakthrough, ancient centres Beliveau and Richard redoubled their efforts. Soon Montreal was taking the game to Chicago. Little Henri scored with time running out in the second, then early in the third, took a feed from Reggie Houle and swung in past a diving Keith Magnuson, deked Esposito, and threw the Cup-winner in the yawning twine. In the team's victorious plane back to Montreal, John Ferguson turned to Beliveau with tears in his eyes and said, "Jean, I can't do it anymore, I think I'm going to retire with you." Surely, Big Jean and Fergy had done enough. The victory marked the fifth time in seven seasons the undervalued '60s edition of the Montreal Canadiens won the Stanley Cup.

FROM RUSSIA WITH LOVE
September 28, 1972

Though not officially an *HNIC* match, game eight of the Super Series was called by Foster Hewitt and aired on CBC. Ironically, the game everybody saw was, before the series, the match no network wanted. CTV, the series TV co-sponsor, had pick of games, and chose the first match. Everyone assumed Canada would win in a walk and game eight would only be watched by bored homemakers. But the Soviets were a superb hockey team and the eighth and deciding game, played in Moscow, was witnessed by two out of every three Canadians — 12.5 million of us in all. The

Penalty-killer Peter Mahovlich stickhandles past a defender before outmaneuvering Vladislav Tretiak to score the clinching goal in Canada's game two Super Series win over the Soviet Union.

Above: the Canadian and Soviet teams moments before Armageddon — game eight of the Super Series in Moscow. Below: another perspective on the most famous goal in Canadian hockey.

game of our life began at noon in St. John's and at 9:30 in the morning in Vancouver. Schoolchildren watched in classrooms or assembly halls. Offices were empty; streets deserted. In the TV department of Toronto's downtown Simpsons store, all two hundred sets were tuned to CBC and surrounded by nervous viewers. And with time running out and the game and series still tied, this is what they heard Foster Hewitt say:

> Savard clears to Stapleton. ... He cleared to the open wing to Cournoyer. HERE'S A SHOT! Henderson makes a wild stab for it, and fell. ... HERE'S ANOTHER SHOT, RIGHT IN FRONT, THEY SCORE!!! HENDERSON SCORES FOR CANADA.

A FOGGY NOTION May 20, 1975

In leading the Philadelphia Flyers to Stanley Cups in 1974 and 1975, goalie Bernie Parent stopped everything he could see. Although, one night in Buffalo, he was beaten by a shot he never saw at all. Nobody did. That evening a sour fog crept into Memorial Auditorium soon after the game began. Occasionally, teams took to the ice and began speed skating in circles to fan away settling vapour banks. By overtime, it was as if they were playing in Heaven's clouds (except for the cursing and slashing). Finally, René Robert, part of Buffalo's fabled French Connection, ended the contest by firing a long slapshot from inside the blueline past Parent. The goalie never flinched. Probably because he didn't have the foggiest notion where the puck was.

Where's the puck? Where's the ice? Where am I? René Robert scores an overtime goal on Bernie Parent in a bank of fog.

AULD LANG SYNE December 31, 1975

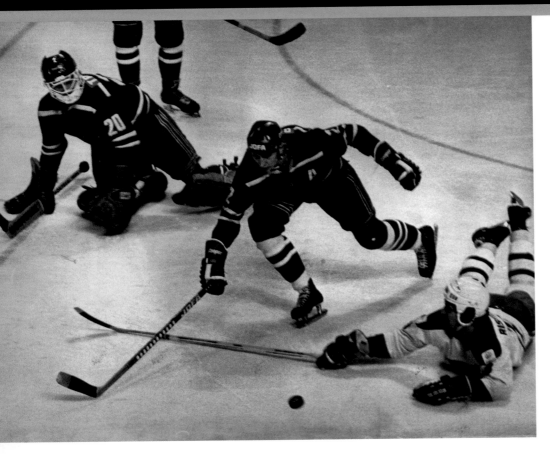

Doug Risebrough throws himself on the ice for a rebound in the justly celebrated Montreal-Red Army New Year's Eve game. Goalie Vladislav Tretiak and Alexander Gusev get their sticks on the ice to ensure the Canadiens forward can't "Henri Richard" the puck into the net.

Canadian hockey fans hadn't forgotten the Red Army team by New Year's 1975. Not with the Russian hero of the 1972 Super Series, Vladislav Tretiak, standing sentry in the Army goal.

Their opponents this evening were *les Glorieux* — the Montreal Canadiens. And the game, which was held before a wildly appreciative Forum audience, is widely considered the best hockey game ever played. The Canadiens, who would go on from here to win four Stanley Cups, began the contest with the energy of colts escaping a burning stable. In the first 10 minutes, the powerful Soviet team failed to get a single puck on Ken Dryden. At the other end, the Habs smothered Tretiak with attention. Steve Shutt scored on a lovely slapshot, and Yvon Lambert slapped in a rebound to make it 2–0 early. After that, the Canadiens had many "glittering" opportunities to swell their lead, according to HNIC's Danny Gallivan. But Tretiak was, to borrow again from the great broadcaster, "simply stupendous." In the third period, the Red Army tied the game on a beautifully choreographed three-on-one, finished off by Lance Corporal Boris Aleksandrov. The game ended in a three-all tie with the Forum crowd shouting approval in the manner of theatre-goers applauding a magnificent entertainment.

THE RUSSIANS ARE LEAVING January 11, 1976

The undefeated Red Army team were finishing off a four-game exhibition tour of North America. Last, but certainly not least, on their itinerary were the Broad Street Bullies — the two-time Stanley Cup champion, Philadelphia Flyers. This was the team of "Mad Dog" Kelly, Andre "Moose" Dupont, Dave the "Hammer" Schultz, and the most combative player of the era, captain Bobby Clarke (who "gave a tickle" to Valery Kharlamov in the 1972 Super Series, breaking the Soviet star's ankle). Early in the first period, the Flyers deported themselves like strikebreakers more than hockey players, cuffing around their opponents at every opportunity. When Ed Van Impe crashed Kharlamov to the ice without drawing a penalty, the Soviet team left the ice for 16 minutes to protest the refereeing. They came back when Flyer management threatened to withhold the Red Army share of the gate. When play resumed, it was the Red Army who were fighting a penalty (for delay of game). Philadelphia scored the first goal, and then breezed to a 4–1 victory. Russian players, who were on the look out for Mooses and Mad Dogs rather than goals this afternoon, were outshot 49–13.

Above: Ed Van Impe (2) attempts to fillet a Red Army forward. Below: the Red Army team leave the ice before the first period is over to protest Philadelphia's bullying tactics. The man holding the mike, and explaining the Army's retreat to folks back home, is "the Russian Foster Hewitt" — Nikolai Ozerov.

TWENTY-SEVEN SCORES TEN February 7, 1976

Above: Darryl Sittler scoring five of his six goals against the Boston Bruins. Bottom right: his final tally, a billiards trick shot off Bruins defenceman Brad Park.

Darryl Sittler probably threw on an old coat that morning and found a twenty-dollar bill in the pocket. It was just his day. Playing at home against Boston later that evening, all the Maple Leaf's industry was blessed. If he threw the puck back to the blueline, defencemen scored (Ian Turnbull and Borje Salming with two); if he dished it to the side, a winger tallied (Lanny McDonald). His own goals came in clumps of three in the second and third period. With his fifth goal (and ninth point), Sittler bettered the single game-point record held by the Rocket and Bert Olmstead. It was Sittler's sixth goal, however, a trick shot worthy of Minnesota Fats, which typified number 27's incredible game. From behind the Boston net, Darryl skimmed a backhand along the ice that bounced off Brad Park's skate, then caromed between goalie Jeff Reese's legs.

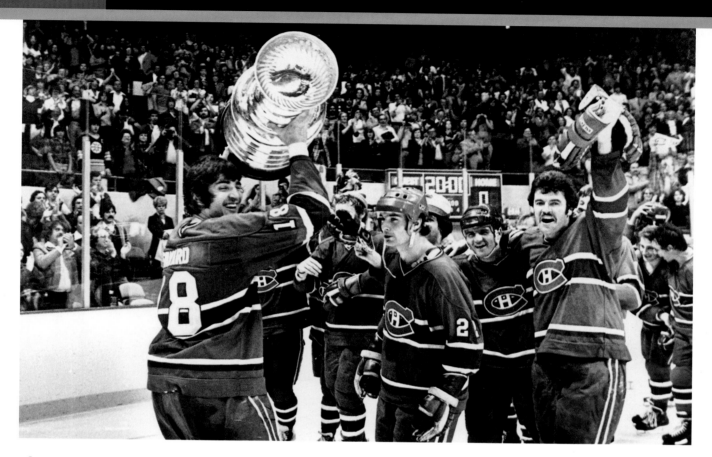

Serge Savard performs a cha-cha-cha with the Stanley Cup. Looking on: Steve Shutt (22), Jacques Lemaire and Yvon Lambert.

If not the best, the 1976–79 edition of the Montreal Canadiens was certainly the most dominant NHL team ever. Over the course of four seasons, the Lafleur-era Canadiens won 229 regular season games, lost 46, and tied 45 on the way to four Stanley Cups.

In the 1976–77 season, the Habs outscored the opposition by better than two-to-one (387–171).

Coach Bowman threw out four lines of fresh, fast forwards: the Shutt-Mahovlich-Lafleur and Wilson-Lemaire-Cournoyer lines piled up big leads; then defensive piranhas Gainey, Roberts, Tremblay, Riseborough and Lambert climbed right inside other team's jerseys.

For opposition forwards who somehow made their way inside the Habs' end, the Montreal net was no more than a rumour behind the huge, mobile defence pairings of Savard-Lapointe and Robinson-Nyrop. Finally, in net there was the 75-inch Dryden.

This year, the Canadiens swept all major awards, with Lafleur winning the MVP and scoring championship. Ken Dryden and Larry Robinson picked up the trophies for best goalie and defence-man.

HABS SHAKE OFF
BLOODY NOSE March 21, 1978

Montreal was supposed to skate all over Boston in the 1978 Cup finals. And sure enough, Lafleur and Co. got off to quick wins at home. But in the sweltering Boston Garden, the Hab blitzkrieg faltered, with Don Cherry's Bruins sweeping two; the second, a penalty-filled 4–3 overtime win. It was a fight in that contest, however, that captured our interest: a second period dustup pitting David (Stan Jonathon) against Goliath (Pierre Bouchard). The players traded furious rights, with little effect, and then Jonathon switched hands, catching Bouchard square on the beak. The defenceman went down immediately, his face raining blood. The incident turned out to be an audition tape for Cherry, who complained when he learned the fight wasn't replayed on TV. Two matches later, a Bruin was KO'd by a Canadien, causing Cherry to storm into HNIC studio, mid-game.

"I guess you're going to replay that one, eh!" Cherry shouted at producer Don Wallace, who explained HNIC never replayed fights. "From that moment on," Wallace told Scott Young, "I sensed here was a guy who wanted to be involved in television." As for the post-fight response from the Canadiens, viewers watched Larry Robinson and Doug Risebrough apply psychological smelling salts to Bouchard and Gilles Lupien (who had tangled unsuccessfully with John Wensink). In the next two games, Montreal played with greater purpose, sweeping the Bruins aside by identical 4–1 scores.

Top: moments before the Jonathon-Bouchard brouhaha, HNIC executive producer Ralph Mellanby, Dave Hodge (laughing, middle) and his frequent playoff foil, Lou Nanne, enjoy a light moment. The bottom three frames capture the action that led to the infamous slugfest.

THE LACROSSE PASS

April 29, 1978

Second only to the mighty Habs in the late '70s, the talented New York Islanders looked to be in for only a modest challenge against the Leafs this playoff season. But with goalie Mike the "Popcorn Kid" Palmateer, Borje Salming, and the Sittler-McDonald-Williams line taking turns playing hero, the Leafs took the Islanders to game seven. Still, the team was having trouble breaking through New York's defence. So Coach Roger Neilson, always an innovator, had Leafs work on firing and accepting high passes in practice.

The game turned out to be a claustrophobic affair, with both teams checking hard. Then, in overtime, Neilson's strategy finally yielded a dividend, as Ian Turnbull surprised the Islanders with a lacrosse pass to Lanny McDonald crossing the New York blueline. Leafs' number seven knocked the puck down with his right hand and chased after it, tipping the puck past Chico Resch for the series-winning goal. Afterward, he tossed his stick and gloves away like a happy kid ridding himself of unwanted garments coming home after school.

Lanny McDonald attempts to hop aboard Darryl Sittler seconds after scoring the overtime goal that sent Toronto into the semi-finals against Montreal. Future Leaf coach Dan Maloney is about to join in the merriment.

FLOWER POWER May 10, 1979

The Flower — Guy Lafleur powers a slapshot past Gilles Gilbert in the dying minutes to send Montreal into overtime against Don Cherry's Boston Bruins.

Though a great club, Don Cherry's Boston Bruins had no business beating Scotty Bowman's Canadiens — arguably hockey's only "perfect team" — in the 1979 semi-finals. Nevertheless, they were leading 4–3 with less than two minutes to go in the seventh, decisive game.

Bruin goalie Gilles Gilbert had been outstanding, and Cherry's heroic proletariat, led by Terry O'Reilly, Brad Park and ace-scorer Rick "Nifty" Middleton (two goals tonight), were outplaying Montreal. The only threat to Boston's sovereignty was Guy Lafleur who found an extra gear in the third period, setting up two goals. Still, dependable checker Don Marcotte kept him scoreless. Boston was in control.

Then a whistle. Too many men on the ice. Boston. HNIC cameras caught Bruins' coach Cherry, who rallied his team while the Forum crowd, smelling blood, let out a scream of wild, military excitement. They knew.

A few shifts later, Lafleur took a pass from Jacques Lemaire and flew at top speed, his hair a blond flag, toward the Bruin end. Almost without breaking stride, he let go a short, swift slapshot inside the blueline. Gilbert kicked. "...*He scores!*" shouted play-by-play man Danny Gallivan.

After plugger Yvon Lambert won the game for Montreal in overtime, Cherry would say of the late penalty that it probably cost his team a Stanley Cup: "It was my fault. The guy couldn't have heard me yell. I grabbed two other guys trying to go over the boards. That would have made eight on the ice. Might as well have let them go."

The Flower in bloom: Canadien folk hero Guy Lafleur in his prime, readying himself for a dash up the ice. "Do you like Guy Lafleur?" Quebec folk singer Robert Charlebois once asked a Montreal crowd. A scream shook Olympic Stadium. "I like him, too," the entertainer smiled. "In the winter, he replaces the sun."

GORDIE SAYS GOODBYE

February 5, 1980

The 1980 NHL all-star game spanned five generations of professional hockey. Held in Detroit, the game marked Wayne Gretzky's first all-star game, and boyhood hero Gordie Howe's 23rd and final exhibition match. The crowd erupted twice in the game — when the 51-year-old legend was introduced, and then later when he was credited with an assist (on a goal by Real Cloutier). By 1980, the laconic, easygoing (off the ice) Howe had been around so long we felt we knew him. Years earlier, Gordie had made a fishing trip to a lake north of Edmonton. Driving across a bridge, Howe saw a man fishing. He slowed the car and rolled down the window. "How they biting?" he asked. The stranger turned to Howe as if he was someone who lived down the street. "Pretty good, Gord," he replied.

Top: Gordie Howe acknowledges the Detroit crowd's stirring ovation at the beginning of the game. The crowd erupted again when Howe assisted on Real Cloutier's goal (bottom frames).

BRINGING HIS GAME UP A NOTCH May 24, 1980

During regulation play, the stars of the great Islander team of the early eighties were almost always the same — Trottier and Bossy upfront, Denis Potvin on the point, and "Battling" Billy Smith in net. But in overtime, the leading player on the four-time Stanley Cup winners was most often "honest" journeyman winger Bob Nystrom, who managed to contribute four playoff overtime goals. "I honestly believed I would score in overtime," Nystrom once said. In fact, before overtime sessions, he followed a dressing-room ritual of carving a notch in his stick in anticipation of a game winner. His most famous "notch," all fans remember, came in the sixth and deciding game of the 1980 finals against the Flyers, when Nystrom, skating hard and hunched in anticipation, directed an expert pass from John Tonelli over Pete Peeters to give the Islanders their first Cup.

Mike Bossy, Denis Potvin (5) and Gord Lane join the wild Islander scrum surrounding overtime hero Bob Nystrom.

The thin blue line. Front row: Brian McFarlane, Don Whitman, Ted Reynolds, Dick Irvin, Bob Cole, Gilles Tremblay, Bill Hewitt, Gerry Pinder, Danny Gallivan.
Back row: Dave Hodge, Lionel Duval, Gary Dornhoeffer, Mickey Redmond, Don Cherry, Steve Armitage, John Wells, Gary Arthur.

THE PASSING
OF THE MICROPHONE

Play-by-play man Bob Cole (middle) is swept away by the action in a Toronto contest. That's *HNIC*'s Greg Millen standing to his left.

Although he hasn't called a game since the late '70s, Foster Hewitt's voice can still be heard on HNIC.

"Foster was my broadcast model," says current play-by-play man and Newfoundland native Bob Cole. "He was the best, and when I was breaking into radio in the fifties, Foster was kind enough to listen to one of my tapes and invited me into his office."

There, the broadcast legend broke down the game of hockey, but not like a coach. Hewitt talked of sport as drama. "One thing he told me," Cole remembers, "is he felt uncomfortable if someone said, 'Foster, you called a great game.' To him the ultimate compliment was, 'Boy, that was a great game.' The game always came first."

Hockey, Hewitt believed, was best served by an announcer who understood drama had an ebb and flow. "Don't yell for 60 minutes," he told Cole. "There is a voice level for a game-winning goal, your top level, and you have to build to it."

Hewitt advised his pupil that every aspect of a broadcast had a different sound. "If a player swept behind his net with the puck on a rush up the boards, your voice climbs with him." Cole also remembers Hewitt saying, "And a player hitting a goal post late in the third period should be translated with a different sense of excitement than a player hitting a goal post early in the game."

Upon returning to St. John's, Cole implemented the lessons of his music teacher. "I would tape my games," he says, "then listen for all the things Foster talked about. ... Gradually, I developed my own style.

"'Don't get in the way of a game,' he said, 'embellish it, heighten the drama ... but let the game play itself.'"

A DREAM COME TRUE

When I was younger, I used to play and broadcast hockey. Some nights I'd play for Bishop Feild College. I was a centre. And when I wasn't playing, I broadcast games, play-by-play. Pretended I was Foster Hewitt.

Anyway, a fellow told me, "You're not bad. You might have a career in this." Well, I knew I wasn't going to make it as a player, so that seemed like a good plan.

Eventually I became a DJ in St. John's at VOCM Radio Newfoundland. This was 1954. I was a kid. I read the news, played music. And I broadcast hockey. Junior, senior, everything. In 1967, HNIC's Ralph Mellanby invited me to tape a game between Montreal and Detroit. I sat in an empty booth in the Forum and away I went. Must have done OK, because in 1969 I got the thrill of my life, doing colour for Foster Hewitt on CBC Sunday hockey broadcasts. What a thrill for a boy from St. John's. Here was Mr. Hockey. And back home we always remembered

Bob Cole

him saying, "Hello hockey fans in Canada *and Newfoundland.*" I got goosebumps being there, I tell you. Foster didn't broadcast hockey, he conducted the flow of the game. He was the best.

I got my big break when they asked me to do play-by-play for a Montreal-Boston Sunday afternoon playoff game. April 24, 1969. Oh, I was nervous. But it was a terrific game. Jean Beliveau scored at 11:28 of the second overtime to win. Maybe because it was a great game, the broadcast went over well. In Montreal, fans listened to the game at Jarry Park, and the batters called time out when they heard a big noise in the crowd. Something happened in the hockey game.

After that, my next big break came in 1972, when I did radio play-by-play for the Canada-Russia series. Funny thing, I asked to come down early so I could learn the Soviet names. I showed up to meet the team day after they arrived. And they thought I was a big-deal Canadian representative. I had dinner with the coach, Bobrov. Charming guy. Went into the dressing room to get lineups. Which was odd. The players all had equipment piled high in the middle of the floor, and they were quiet, grim almost. Nothing like Canadian players.

Anyway, that series was the highlight of my career. And it opened the door to doing hockey on TV. It's all been terrific. I tell people my career on HNIC has been a dream come true. *Bob Cole*

STAYING IN THE GAME

Harry Neale as a Junior Marlie back when the world was young.

I was born in Sarnia, Ontario, and, like a lot of Canadian kids, I grew up wanting to play NHL hockey. Working on HNIC has given me a chance to stay in the game right up to the Stanley Cup every season. That's something no coach or player could possibly hope for, not with 30 teams playing every year.

How did I get my start in hockey broadcasting? While I was coaching the Vancouver Canucks, Don Wallace, executive producer of HNIC at the time, said to me, "When you get fired, come work for me." Then I moved to Detroit to coach the Red Wings. I was eventually fired — on a Thursday — in 1985. The next day, I phoned Don and said, "OK, I'm ready."

I was on television that Saturday night. I showed up with no experience, not knowing what to do. You could do that then. I did a couple of games and what must have been a horrific job the first few times. The next year, John Davidson took over as the person in charge of staffing commentators and, lo and behold, I found myself working full-time as a hockey colour commentator.

How has the job changed over the years? There are certainly more refinements to the telecasts now — slow mo, swinging lights, isolation. You get used to thinking that you have to replay something every time you hear a whistle. You haven't even seen the replay yourself, but you have to make it sound as if you've seen it.

But I don't want to make it sound like the job is too tough. To tell you the truth, I never considered working on HNIC to be a job at all. *Harry Neale*

TONGUE LASHINGS

Harry Neale's tongue is the rare instrument that grows sharper with use.

A star with the Toronto Junior Marlboros in the mid-fifties, Neale coached in college and junior hockey before becoming coach and GM of the Vancouver Canucks in the late '70s. And this is where, in self-defence really, the veteran hockey man perfected his gift for sharp-as-a-skate one-liners.

"We can't win on the road and we can't win at home. My failure as a coach is I can't think of anywhere else to play," was one famous rebuke. Another: "I knew I was in trouble when I heard my best forward say to my best defenceman, 'I always have a bad game when I hear that song' and it was the national anthem."

Arriving at HNIC, Neale's cold-water wit brought him instant celebrity. Vintage Neale slapshots:

Puckish wit Harry Neale

"This is an East-West game and Hartford is playing for the North."

"That's Kraig Nienhaus. Looks like he combs his hair with a hand grenade."

Where does Harry get them? Well, he collects pithy observations, and then waits, sometimes for years, for the right moment.

Arguably, Neale's best lines are a good critic's response to admirable or bad play. Like the night Stephane Richer wouldn't give up the puck in a quixotic dash to the Leafs' net:

"Stephane likes to stickhandle, doesn't he?" Harry responded with a sigh. "If someone opened the player gate, he would have tried to fake out an usher."

A COMING-OUT PARTY

April 11, 1981

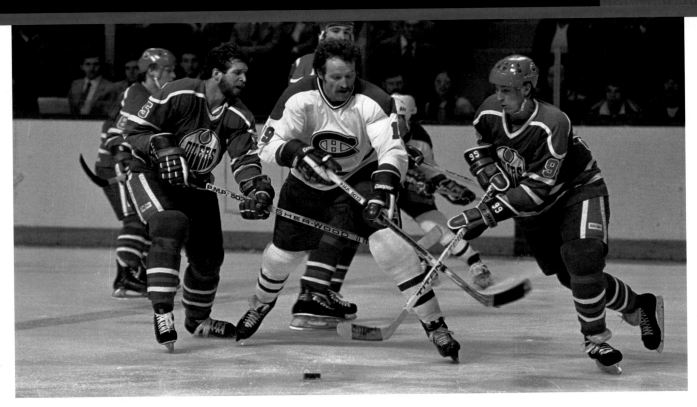

God must've been whispering in the Edmonton Oiler management's ears between 1978 and 1981. In those seasons, the Oilers

Wayne Gretzky crosses Habs stalwart Larry Robinson. Gretzky would score 21 points in nine playoff games in this, his second NHL playoff campaign.

retained the rights to Wayne Gretzky and without ever managing a top-5 draft pick, nabbed Kevin Lowe (21), Mark Messier (48) and Glenn Anderson (69) in 1979; Paul Coffey (6), Jari Kurri (69) and Andy Moog (132) in 1980; and Grant Fuhr (8) and Steve Smith (111) in 1981. The team finished 14th in 1981, but 20-year-old Gretzky led the league in scoring. Everyone agreed Edmonton was a team of great promise, but no one guessed that the promise would come true in these playoffs, against the formidable Lafleur-Robinson-era Canadiens.

In the first period of game one, Gretzky threw touchdown passes to Anderson and Kurri (two) to go up 3–1. But it was during the break that the Oilers really showed their stuff. Someone said to Messier it looked as if he almost got in a fight with the immortal Robinson. Mess shook his head. "I'm going to wait till I get him against the boards and then I'm going to beat the crap out of him!" he promised, exhibiting the bristling conceit of a champion. Oilers won the game 6–2 and the series 3–0. The experienced Islanders took Edmonton in the next round, and brought home Cups in 1982 and 1983. But it was clear after the team's first playoff win in Montreal that Gretzky's Oilers were next in line for the throne.

WHITE-HOT CANUCKS

April 29, 1982

When future *HNIC* colour man Harry Neale was suspended as coach of the Vancouver Canucks in 1982, assistant Roger Neilson took over. The Canucks weren't supposed to go anywhere in the playoffs, but they gained momentum and confidence as the postseason continued, upsetting first Calgary, and then Los Angeles before facing Chicago in the semi-finals.

It was against the Hawks that Roger Neilson cemented his reputation as a mischief-maker.

Above, far left: Vancouver Canucks coach Roger Neilson offers mock surrender to officials, waving a bench towel with a stick. Next frame, we see Canuck players, including Dave "Tiger" Williams, join in what would be an expensive protest. Irate officials then gave Roger the heave-ho, ejecting him from the game. Neilson (below) would eventually lead the Canucks to the Stanley Cup finals.

Neilson had been apprenticing for the role a long time; as a Toronto baseball coach (Ken Dryden was one of his players), he designed a play that had the catcher throwing a peeled apple over the third basemen's head, drawing the runner home, where he was calmly tagged out by the catcher.

His chicanery in the semi-finals was comparatively modest, but successful. Upset with refereeing, he waved a white towel, conceding defeat to the officials. Then Tiger Williams followed suit, as did Harold Snepts. Canucks were fined $10,000 for the gesture, but next game in Vancouver the entire Pacific Coliseum arena was bright with white, waving towels.

The white-hot Canucks, with goalie Richard Brodeur playing the hockey of his life, eventually made it into the finals before surrendering to the powerful Trottier-Bossy-Potvin Islanders.

THE NATURAL February 8, 1983

The eyes have it: more than any player before or since, Wayne Gretzky could see a play developing before anyone else. Here, he maps out an attack early in his career.

Some think Wayne Gretzky became a bona fide North American hockey celebrity when he scored four goals in the third period of the 1983 all-star game in New York. Then, after overwhelming his opponents, Gretzky completely won over the America media, playing a role that seemed to come naturally: a gracious 22-year-old superstar made humble by the gift that had been bestowed upon him.

By then, however, Canadian fans knew all about Wayne. In 1982, there was a great deal of speculation whether Gretzky could break the Rocket's record of 50 goals in 50 games. By the 38th game, he had 41 goals; nine goals in 12 games seemed possible. It wouldn't take that long, as it turned out. "We played back-to-back games," remembers teammate Paul Coffey. "[That morning] he says, 'I think I'm going to get four tonight.' Well, he goes out and gets four. The next morning, on the way to breakfast, he says, 'I think I'm going to get five tonight.' I say, 'Yeah, whatever.' And he got five goals."

Gretzky was hockey's great Natural, a miracle of co-ordination and competitive courage. And yet he was so slender and frail, coach John Muckler remembers, "When Wayne won his first Stanley Cup [in 1984], he had trouble holding it in the air, like he was almost afraid he'd fall over backward."

Danse macabre: members of the Quebec Nordiques and Montreal Canadiens size up their partners during an interlude of the "Good Friday Massacre."

Old-time fans insist it started in 1915 when a Quebec Bulldog snapped Canadien star Newsy Lalonde's collarbone. The resulting rivalry, they say, only worsened when the Habs stole Jean Beliveau and Guy Lafleur from Quebec City decades later. Historians, however, suggest the feud was always there, pointing out that Montreal was founded over the howling protests of Quebec City citizens, who wanted de Maisonneuve to build a new community on Ile d'Orléans.

In any case, when the Nordiques joined the NHL in 1979, the Montreal-Quebec City conflict became an epic hockey rivalry. During playoffs, the Battle for Quebec was nothing less than a seven-game war. Though the Habs finished 27 points up on Les Nords in 1982, Dale Hunter's goal eliminated Montreal in a game-five overtime. And, in 1985, Peter Stastny scored in an identical circumstance to kill Montreal's playoff hopes. The Habs, however, won three playoffs, twice going on to win the Stanley Cup. All these battles were marked by fights and violent mood swings. (Quebec City was conflicted in these affairs because native sons Guy Lafleur and Patrick Roy starred for *le bleu-blanc-rouge*.) The rivalry spun out of control during the "Good Friday Massacre," a 1984 bench-clearing playoff brawl.

The Battle for Quebec ended in 1995, when Quebec became Colorado — but the Montreal-Quebec City rivalry never died. In 2002, the Avalanche held an exhibition game against Montreal in the Colisée. Seats disappeared two hours after going on sale. When Joe Sakic, a former Nordique, entered the arena wearing Nordique blue, the fans gave him a thunderous ovation. "I was here seven years," Sakic would say of his reception. "You're not going to find a better hockey city. It was really moving. There are no words."

MURDER IN ALBERT'R

April 30, 1986

Teammate Don Jackson comforts Steve Smith after the Oiler defenceman inadvertently fired the puck into his own net. Smith would redeem himself with exemplary play in subsequent Oiler playoffs.

In the '80s, the Crown and Anchor Pub, a bar in Red Deer, Alberta, drew a line down the middle of the floor to separate Edmonton Oilers and Calgary Flames fans watching HNIC. A sensible plan, given that the sight of a rival's jersey left players and fans seeing red (even if they were looking at Oiler blue and orange). Once in the playoffs, Edmonton's Marty McSorley tangled with Calgary's Doug Risebrough. In the penalty box, Risebrough discovered an Edmonton jersey in his hands and stomped it to used-car-lot ribbons, then tossed it out on the ice.

Losing was a crying matter in these playoffs. And almost always, Calgary's fans ended up shedding the tears, because the Oilers, led by redoubtable netminder Grant Fuhr, and the opportunistic sniping of Gretzky, Kurri, Messier et al., always emerged victorious.

The one exception was in the spring of 1986, when in the third period of game seven, Edmonton defender Steve Smith swung behind his net in search of a breaking winger. Unfortunately, his clearing pass hit the back of Fuhr's leg. When the goalie turned, even his mask looked surprised to find the puck in the net with what turned out to be the winning goal.

THE SHOT April 21, 1988

Wayne Gretzky could do anything that needed to be done to win. As a 10-year-old boy, he won MVP in an Ontario bantam baseball tournament, playing shortstop and pitching for his Brantford team. He threw a no-hitter one game with his right arm, and then later in the tourney, growing weary, turned around and pitched with his left arm.

On the ice, Wayne could do everything with a puck better than anyone else, except he really didn't have a great slapshot. Nevertheless, in overtime of game two in the 1988 Calgary-Edmonton playoffs, the Oiler captain found the puck with open ice down the left boards and took off in his familiar hunched-over, elbows-digging skating style. Between the Calgary blueline and faceoff circle he wound up quickly, slapping a blur over the shoulder of Mike Vernon for what was the decisive goal in the series.

After beating the Flyers in a subsequent round to win the Stanley Cup, Gretzky flung the trophy over his head, sending the home crowd in the Northlands Coliseum into ecstasy. Then, in one of the most memorable moments in playoff history, the captain turned to give the trophy to Steve Smith, pained victim of the team's playoff defeat the previous year.

The shot that doused the Flames: Gretzky beats Mike Vernon on a high slapshot. In the last frame, Gretzky accepts congratulations from Mike Krushelnyski and Craig Simpson.

LE ROI May 24, 1986

It seemed impossible that a French-Canadian goalie could have more descendants than Georges the "Chicoutimi Cucumber" Vezina, who sired 22 children. And yet, Patrick Roy, a third-round draft pick from Ste. Foy, Quebec, has spawned at least that many imitators in his native province. By 2003, three of the final four semi-final Stanley Cup goalies, J.S. Giguere, Martin Brodeur and Manny Fernandez were Quebec clones of *Le Roi*.

No one has ever been able to cover the lower portion of the net better than Patrick Roy. Here, the Montreal star goes low to block an effort from tobogganing winger Lanny McDonald.

Roy received his crown — and the first of a record three Conn Smythe playoff MVPs — in the spring of 1986, when he frustrated, one after the other, Boston, Hartford, New York and Calgary. Against New York one playoff night, he blocked 13 straight overtime tries, many seemingly sure goals, before Claude Lemieux scored on Montreal's first shot.

And so it went through the playoffs, as Patrick displayed what became trademark tics — rotating his head as if to resolve a crick in his neck during a lull in play, arguing with goal posts, and, on the rare occasions opponents scored, searching his overabundant sweater and pads for security breaches.

Soon, most goalies would adopt Roy's butterfly style — a modified Glenn Hall stance — to seal the bottom half of the net.

Though often imitated, no one could duplicate Patrick Roy.

THE GAME THAT COULDN'T END April 18–19, 1987

Pat LaFontaine tries to score in the longest-ever NHL game. In the seventh period, the following day, he eventually would.

Playoff hockey is the only televised sport that requires real physical endurance. *HNIC* throws on double headers some spring nights, and if the Western game goes deep into overtime, wives can find their husbands rigid on the couch, a sphinx of potato-chip dust in the morning.

The longest-overtime-ever found the New York Islanders and Washington Capitals playing themselves into dishrags for seven periods. *HNIC*'s Kelly Hrudey played for New York and once reflected on that seventh and deciding game in *Hockey Digest*:

> I was amazed at the pace of the game and how hard the guys worked. It would seem a guy was exhausted and could barely lumber back to the bench, but next shift he would pounce over the boards and give it all he had again.
>
> I never got tired, but my feet hurt. I wear tight skates, and after a normal game, they hurt, but this was beyond being sore.

Finally! Jubilant teammates surround overtime hero Pat LaFontaine.

I could sense more than anything that the fans were thoroughly enjoying the game. Give them a lot of credit, they didn't leave despite the hour. As the game progressed, they became hockey fans rather than just Capitals fans.

When Patty LaFontaine finally scored, there was no buildup. That's how those goals are scored. I remember Gordie Dineen circling the net, with Dale Henry in front creating havoc. Then Patty turned around and shot without even looking.

Then the red light was on. My first reaction was disbelief. I thought, "No, this game can't end, we've been playing this long. There must be a penalty, a man in the crease." But then I realized it was over and I remember jumping without any energy and Randy Boyd coming to hug me and knocking me over.

MURPHY'S PLAYOFFS

'88 Playoffs

It was a playoff year where everything that could go wrong, did. HNIC rookie announcer Chris Cuthbert was dispatched to Washington to file game reports from the Capitals-New York Islander series, but then a power failure in the Montreal Forum left him doing a hockey broadcast entirely by himself, as HNIC switched to the Washington feed. Later in the playoffs, New Jersey coach Jim Schoenfeld became irate after what he felt was a bad call and chased after referee Don Koharski, bellowing, "Have another donut, you fat pig." The league suspended Schoenfeld. But the Devils secured a temporary restraining order to overturn the ruling. When NHL officials refused to participate in the next game with Schoenfeld behind the bench, amateur referees were recruited, two of whom wore what appeared to be yellow long johns. (The game, which was played on Mother's Day, would from here after be referred to as Yellow Sunday.) Finally, in the Stanley Cup finals, a game between Boston and Edmonton was suspended because of a power failure.

Could things possibly get any worse? For Canadian hockey fans in general, and Edmonton Oiler fans in particular, absolutely. In the off-season, the Cup winners did the unthinkable, trading Wayne Gretzky to Los Angeles.

Game footage from Yellow Sunday, when replacement officials — some of whom appeared to be wearing yellow long johns — were forced into action to handle the New Jersey-Boston semi-finals. The linesman and referee nearly collide in the second frame. Below: New Jersey coach (and freelance donut salesman) Jim Schoenfeld.

Lanny lugs the Cup: Captain Lanny McDonald skates off with Calgary's first-ever Stanley Cup. Trailing Flames include Joel Otto (29), Joe Nieuwendyk (25) and Haken Loob (12).

Like a great fighter who competed in an era dominated by an overwhelming champion, Calgary Flames never received their due because of the Gretzky-Messier Oilers. But in the spring of 1989, with the Great One safely tucked away in Los Angeles, the Flames were not to be denied. A big, mobile defence, led by Al MacInnis, Mike Vernon's timely goaltending, and strong work upfront by Doug Gilmour, Joey Mullen and strong-as-an-oak centre Joel Otto, gave the Flames a 3–2 lead going into game six in Montreal. Then, early in the third period of a fiercely contested two-all game, the pride of Hanna, Alberta, Lanny McDonald, bolted from the penalty box to take a nicely feathered pass from Joe Nieuwendyk and snapped a quick wrist shot over Patrick Roy's shoulder to give Calgary its first championship. Montreal fans, witnessing the loss of the Stanley Cup on home ice for the first time ever, were particularly gracious, giving the Flames a standing ovation at the end of the game. Then the party started. "I was telling the fellas I scored my first one here and wouldn't it be great if I got my last one [in the Forum]," shouted Lanny from behind a prospector's mustache in what would be his final game. MacInnis, named playoff MVP, responded to a question from HNIC's Ron MacLean by howling, "Port Hood, Cape Breton, I love ya' — *whooo-whoo!*"

99 PASSES 9

Wayne Gretzky always set his sights high. His boyhood hero was hockey's greatest scorer, Gordie Howe, whom he first encountered at a hockey tournament as child. The meeting was documented with a photo that reveals Gordie might have seen young Wayne as a potential rival. He's shown hooking the embryonic superstar's head down for closer inspection. As many predicted, Gretzky eventually passed his boyhood hero's greatest record, scoring his 1,851 career point while playing for the Los Angeles Kings. Gordie was on hand to once again pose for pictures with his long-time admirer. Wayne would go on to record more than 1,000 more points, finishing with 2,857 goals and assists.

Above: Gordie Howe takes a professional interest in his heir apparent at a Brantford, Ontario, hockey banquet in 1971. Below: 18 years later, the Great Ones meet again.

117

THE BEST GIFT

He was big, graceful and superbly co-ordinated — the author of 133 goals and 149 assists his last year in junior (Laval Titan). Even his name — Lemieux, "the best" in French — seemed a guarantee of glory. What a shock, then, when Mario arrived at the Pittsburgh Penguins training camp in the fall of 1984 and finished dead last in testing for strength and fitness. Didn't matter, it turned out — Mario was the perfect hockey specimen, deceptively fast, impossible to catch in stride, with a 17-foot wingspan that allowed him to glide past grasping defenders. That he and Gretzky were in the same league (sometimes on the same line for Canada in international competition) seemed like a gift from the hockey gods. By the late '80s, Lemieux reached his prime, scoring 85 goals and 114 assists in the 1989–90 season. Showing off a little, he also tossed in four goals in the 1990 NHL all-star game.

Super Mario lands with an all-star goal after flying through downcast defender Doug Wilson and goalie Mike Vernon. That's Al Iafrate in the bottom right hand corner.

THE BOSTON MARATHON

May 15, 1990

Charlie Huddy (22) and Petr Klima (85) check the Stanley Cup to make sure there's enough room for the 1989–90 Oilers.

It was a game the losers should have won. Boston, led by Ray Bourque and Cam Neely, outplayed Edmonton, outshooting their opponents 31–16 in regular play, yet needed two late goals by Bourque for a tie. Surely, they'd win this, the first game of the 1990 finals, in extra time. The chances were certainly there in the first, second and third overtime. But so too was goalie Bill Ranford, who at one point tortured the Garden crowd by stopping a shot ticketed for an otherwise empty top corner with the knob of his hockey stick. A period later, Glen Wesley hurried a backhand over a yawning net. By the third overtime and sixth hour of hockey, the Boston crowd was all groaned out when Jari Kurri swung into the Bruin zone, and then dropped a pass to an unfamiliar teammate, who whistled a quick, low shot between the legs of Boston goalie Andy Moog. The dancing, celebrating stranger, it turned out, was Petr Klima, out enjoying his first overtime shift of the night.

CAN'T-MESS OILERS May 24, 1990

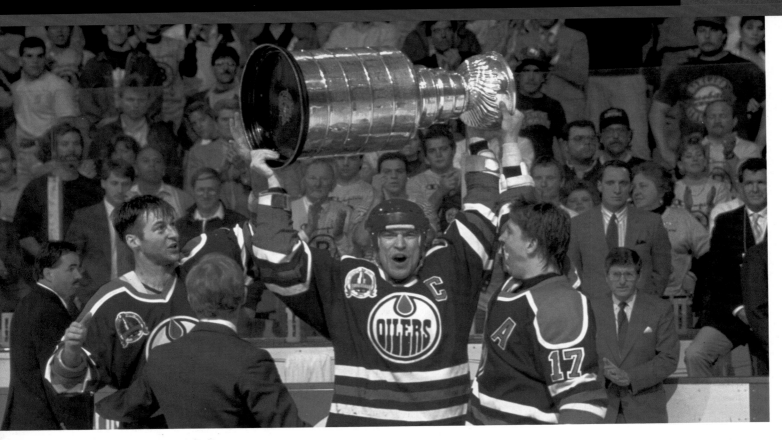

Once more with feeling! Captain Mark Messier, with assists from Kevin Lowe and Jari Kurri (17), hoists the last of five Edmonton Oiler Stanley Cups.

The '80s Oilers reprised all we knew to be great about hockey. Like Punch Imlach, GM/coach Glen Sather was a wise guy who could get under the skin of a turtle; goalie Grant Fuhr's play recalled the heroic playoff stands of Terry Sawchuk; the skittish Paul Coffey, when on, was close as we may ever see to Bobby Orr; while Glenn Anderson, Gretzky and Jari Kurri moved with the speed and grace of the great Habs teams. But maybe the glue that held the team together was Mark Messier, the scowling centre who might have been a stand-in for Charlton Heston in *Ben Hur*. In the spring of 1990, with Gretzky, Fuhr and Coffey absent, Messier confirmed his place in Oiler history, delivering the team its fifth Stanley Cup in seven years while scoring 9 goals and 22 assists in 22 playoff games. Mess and linemates Anderson and Craig Simpson scored 10 points in a 5–1, game-four Stanley Cup final win in Edmonton. Then, in the next Cup-clinching game, Anderson and Simpson tallied early in Boston's beehive — Bruins gave yellow T-shirts prior to the game — for a lead goalie Bill Ranford never relinquished. Afterward, Messier expressed solidarity with Edmonton teams of the past by shouting into *HNIC* microphones, "This one's for you, Gretz."

1990–91 to Present

OUR FAVOURITE CORNER

Ron MacLean and his go-to (or is that goatee?) partner Don Cherry, on *Coach's Corner*, 2003.

They are definitely an odd pair of socks.

The first time Don Cherry put on a headset to cover hockey for U.S. TV, the former Boston Bruin coach got into trouble with his producer.

"Who's gonna win the game?" his on-air partner asked.

"I'll tell ya' if this guy quits yelling in my ear," Cherry groused.

By comparison, Ron MacLean fit into broadcasting before he started shaving. He had a CBC Radio show in Red Deer, Alberta, at age 15. A decade later, as TV weatherman in Calgary, he gained renown for being able to ad lib his way out of any broadcast storm. A hockey addict, he jumped at the chance to join *Hockey Night in Canada*.

By then, Cherry had made TV history as a commentator on HNIC's *Coach's Corner*. And all Don needed was one TV lesson from boss Ralph Mellanby. "First game, 1980, someone asked me something, I go, 'Well, I think such and such …'" Cherry recalls. "Ralph came in all mad later and said, 'You don't think, you *know*! Give it to 'em straight.'"

Weeks later, Don was on air with Danny Gallivan during a dull game. "What do you think, Don?" Gallivan asked.

"Keeps going like this, the Zamboni driver is gonna be first star," Cherry replied.

Sartorial overkill only made Cherry's plain virtues more apparent. Here was an authentic, rarely heard TV voice whose thunderous exclamations and complaints transported us to Thunder Bay and Medicine Hat taprooms, hockey's parish churches.

But it took the arrival of MacLean in 1986 to make *Coach's Corner* a lifelong viewing habit. For, if the essence of drama is conflict, here were sparring partners capable of generating at least 20 years of creative tension.

Sitting down with Cherry in HNIC's green room after *Coach's Corner*, it only takes 10 minutes before the coach shows you how to take a guy out in a fight. "Punch below the eyebrow," Cherry says. "Cuts easy. They bleed, you win."

MacLean later acknowledges that backing down from a midget fight ended his hockey career. "I'd hurt my thumb playing football," he remembers. "But I didn't really want to fight. I was in the wrong place at the wrong time. The seventies was the era of the Broad Street Bullies in Philly, and Alberta was the roughest junior hockey in Canada."

Although Cherry and MacLean are gifted conversationalists, their language and customs are from different eras.

"How come, you go in a supermarket, you're looking for hamburger, it's in metric or something," Don once told us. "But then say a killer is loose, *oh yeah*, then it's OK for the press to say he's six-foot-two, two hundred pounds. Geez, that metric stuff drives me nuts."

Conversely, MacLean enjoys alliterative puns and is a staunch advocate of a modern, pluralistic Canada. His closing words to banquet crowds are usually, "We're not here to see through each other, we're here to see each other through."

How is it Don never tried to poke Ron one in the eyebrow? You wonder.

"Well, we've been through so much by now, battling common enemies, we're friends," MacLean says. "And I love so much about Don. His mischief and the way he punches holes through pomposity. We get into fights on air; off air, too. And Don always seems to be in trouble. But, you know, maybe that's what keeps the show going."

The two men have been partners for so long now, MacLean admits he sometimes has to remind himself not to let their TV work become too private and self-referential.

That must be hard. For off air, in *HNIC*'s green room, the two men carry on as if they're still on air.

"Hey," Cherry says to an assistant, munching on a cookie. "When you send out promo shots of me and Ron, use last year's shots, eh? Look at him here in his white jacket — *gyanahh*."

"Ron said it's easy to autograph in the white," the publicist says.

"But he looks like a waiter."

Cherry bites his lip, trying not to smile. "You wonder I'm the way I am, working with a guy like that," he says.

EIGHT MILLION EYES

Let's go back to May 1993, game seven, Toronto Maple Leafs versus my Los Angeles Kings, with the winner advancing on to play the Montreal Canadiens for the oldest and toughest prize of all — the Stanley Cup. (See story, page 127.)

Putting on our equipment prior to the warmup, we talked about many things in our cramped little dressing room. To me, the most significant aspect to the game was that here we were at Maple Leaf Gardens playing a game that would be shown across the country on HNIC. I momentarily forget about Doug Gilmour and Wendel Clark, two of the toughest competitors we would face that night. Instead, I began thinking about the four million viewers on HNIC who would be cheering and moaning, laughing and crying, over this crucial game the same way I did growing up in Edmonton, watching hockey every Saturday night.

Left-right: Scott Russell, guest Catriona LeMay Doan and Kelly Hrudey from a HNIC "After Hours" segment at the Calgary Saddledome following one of HNIC's regular Saturday night double-headers.

I certainly had no idea that one day I would be on HNIC as an analyst. Yet only two years after my appearance in the finals, the show's executive producer John Shannon asked if I would be interested in making my broadcasting debut on HNIC. My emotions ranged from excitement, nervousness, and pride to fear.

My very first show on HNIC reminded me of two things: the significance the show had on me as a child and the bond the show creates for Canadians from coast to coast to coast because of our deep passion for the sport. Oh boy, was I nervous.

Still, what impresses me the most, though, is the fact that even with the most accomplished broadcasters our country has ever seen — giants like Hewitt, Gallivan, Irvin, Meeker, Cole, MacLean and Cherry — the show's number one priority is the game itself, not the broadcast personalities.

Across this wide land, Canadians continue to tune in each Saturday night and it's our responsibility to tell the players' stories to their greatest fans. *Kelly Hrudey*

AT LAST, FLYING PENGUINS May 25, 1991

Penguins pose with the Stanley Cup.

The Pittsburgh Penguins didn't exactly get off to a flying start. In the team's first season, 1967–68, the Penguins employed a skating penguin, Pete, as rink (the Igloo) mascot. Pete never took to hockey, however, and quit the team late that season with pneumonia. After that, for the next 23 years, the Penguins, like Pete, retired prematurely every spring. Even after Mario Lemieux arrived, the Penguins remained a flightless bird. Then, without warning, having finished out of the playoffs eight of nine previous seasons, Pittsburgh became the best team in hockey in 1991. Lemieux was the primary reason, recovering from injuries to score 44 playoff points. But the team also benefited from the addition of Ron Francis and Junior Mario — rookie Jaromir Jagr — who performed with a mullet hairdo that fell like a wreath past his shoulders. Swift, creative Paul Coffey was on defence along with Ulf Samuelsson. Tom Barrasso provided timely goaltending. And Badger Bob Johnson, for years the Flames luckless coach, schemed and cajoled from behind the Pittsburgh bench. The Penguins flew to victory that spring in spectacular fashion, taking Minnesota 8–0 for a sixth-game victory that gave the team its first Stanley Cup. The next season, with much the same cast, and Scotty Bowman at the helm, Pittsburgh captured its second Cup in a row.

GRET VS. GRIT May 29, 1993

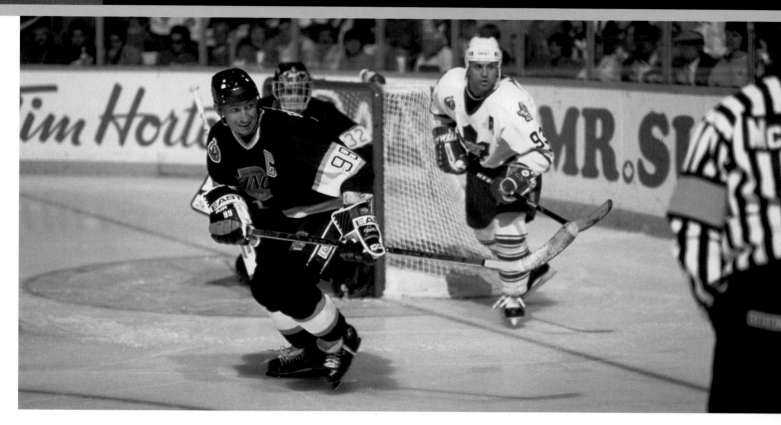

There have been more talented teams, but in 36 years, no Toronto club came closer to a Stanley Cup than the '93 Maple Leafs. This was Doug Gilmour's team. Despite daily carloads of pasta, the "Killer" was down to 160 pounds after a seven-game

No one likes a Killer trailing them. Wayne Gretzky speeds away from Doug Gilmour. Future HNIC broadcaster Kelly Hrudey looks on from the safety of his goal cage.

playoff series against Detroit and St. Louis. Every shift in these semi-finals with Los Angeles he gave more than he had, and then fell to the bench, seemingly haggard beyond repair, only to spring back when coach Pat Burns called his number. It was also Wendel Clark's team. The captain scored 10 goals these playoffs, including a hat trick in a losing effort, game six. Other contributors included Felix "The Cat" Potvin, along with veteran muckers "Krusher" Krushelnyski and Mike Foligno.

On the other side, the Kings had future *HNIC* colour man Kelly Hrudey, wearing a series of festive bandanas, in net, and Wayne Gretzky quarterbacking a West Coast offence. The Leafs were on the verge of conquering L.A. a dozen times, only to have Gretzky bring his team back in some improbable manner. In game seven, number 99 killed Toronto's hopes of a finals showdown against Montreal, with a dastardly pool shot, caroming a puck off defencemen Dave Ellett's skate past Potvin from behind the net.

NEW YORK'S OILERS BEAT CANUCKS June 14, 1994

Benchmark of success: the New York Rangers leap to the ice to celebrate the team's first championship since 1940.

The last hurrah for the great Edmonton team of the '80s came in 1994, when the New York Rangers, with a sextet of ex-Oilers defeated the mulishly stubborn Vancouver Canucks. Vancouver goalie Kirk McLean stole the first game in the finals in New York, but Rangers came back to win three straight. Series over, it was thought. New York, which had not seen the Rangers win a Cup since 1940, even set the date for a victory parade. Then Pavel Bure and Trevor Linden rudely went on scoring sprees, helping to beat the Rangers 6–3 and 4–1 in games five and six.

The seventh contest, played in Madison Square Garden, was an electric affair, with New York jumping to an early 2–0 lead. Linden, however, silenced the home crowd with a shorthanded goal early in the second. Mark Messier restored order with a third Ranger goal, only to have Linden make it close again with a goal early in the third. After that, it was hectic, jittery hockey. Nelson LaFayette frightened all Manhattan by wobbling a loose puck off the post behind Mike Richter with five minutes left. The remaining seconds were agony for both teams' fans, with three faceoffs in the New York end in the last 37 seconds.

The final faceoff came with two seconds left. Ex-Oilers Messier and Craig MacTavish conferred and came up with a gambit to ensure victory. Figuring officials wouldn't call a penalty at such a dramatic moment, both Rangers committed fouls on the final drop of the puck, as first Messier then MacTavish whacked and cross-checked Pavel Bure. The siren and crowd's screams silenced the Russian Rocket's protests. In delivering the Rangers their first Stanley Cup in 54 years, Messier became a folk hero in New York.

THE KING ABDICATES

December 2, 1995

The last Canadien hero, Patrick Roy, began his career with the worst junior team in Canada — the Granby Bisons — where his goals against average hovered around five. But even there he played with something close to valour. So the Canadiens took a chance on the goalie in the 1984 draft.

Performing in the hallowed Forum with a diligent supporting class, Roy became the best goalie in the world. In early 1993, he put on a legendary post-season stand, posting 10 consecutive overtime wins against Quebec, Buffalo, the Islanders and Los Angeles, in winning Montreal the Stanley Cup.

In most of these games, Roy was the best player on the ice. That he always spoke his mind and was highly visible in the off-season, representing the Canadiens (and himself) at an endless string of charity sporting events, made him a hero of the Quebec people in the manner of Rocket Richard and Guy Lafleur.

Roy had the temperament of a Richard as well. In late 1995, the goalie was left to languish in net by coach (and ex-roommate) Mario Tremblay for nine goals in a humiliating 11–1 HNIC Saturday night loss to Detroit. Pulled late in the game, the fuming goalie fixed his coach with a gelid stare, and then walked to club president Ronald Corey, seated behind the bench, and announced, "That's my last game in Montreal."

Soon he would be traded to Colorado (the old Nordiques!). "I had a 10-year love affair with the Montreal Canadiens and it ended in heartbreak," Roy later told a reporter.

Top: Patrick Roy lifts his arms in mock celebration after making a save in a humiliating 11–1 loss to Detroit. Subsequent frames find him exchanging a look as cold as the Forum ice with coach Mario Tremblay. Afterward, he tells club president Ronald Corey he's through, and then sits fuming on the bench.

Tearful goodbye: the Jets say goodbye to Winnipeg.

By the time the Winnipeg Jets landed in Phoenix in 1996, Jet fans' hearts were beyond repair. The franchise had some great moments. Three seasons they'd been World Hockey Association champs. And no Winnipegger could forget Bobby Hull playing on the Luxury Line with Christian Bordeleau and Normie Beaudin (or better still, Ulf Nilsson and Anders Hedberg). Then came a cruel NHL initiation: 30 games in a row without victory in 1980. All that futility at least gave them first pick in next year's draft: Dale Hawerchuk.

Five seasons later, in the spring of 1985, the Jets pulled off an inspiring playoff win over Calgary. The victory that came with a price tag, however. The great Hawerchuk broke a rib. As a result, Jets were easy prey for Edmonton next round.

Oh, the cursed Oilers! In the '80s, Winnipeg went 1–18 against the lordly Albertans in different playoff seasons. Finally, in the spring of 1990, Winnipeg had Edmonton where they wanted them, up three games to one, thanks to a memorable Dave Ellett double-overtime goal. But Edmonton clawed back, winning in seven games. Then, more heartache: The Finnish Flash, Teemu Selanne, came and went. (With the Jets, the teeter-totter always seemed to stay down longer than up.)

Winnipeg was again valiant in a final, six-game, 1996 playoff stand against overpowering Detroit. But in the end, they lost. Again. The long goodbye that followed — the Jets circling the ice to thank shouting fans for their support, with both parties knowing the team was bound for Phoenix — was the final heartbreak.

PUCKINGHAM PALACE

November 11, 1931

Never one to shrink from a challenge, Leaf owner Conn Smythe built an ice palace in the teeth of the Depression. Scraping together $1.2 million in financing, the sand-and-gravel tycoon hurriedly hired on construction crews, only to discover the cheapest contract tender was for $1.5 million. Assistant Frank Selke, Sr., saved the day — and rink — by convincing labourers to accept shares in the new arena, which was thrown together in less than six months. Over the years, Maple Leaf Gardens would acquire numerous nicknames, from The House That Smythe Built to the Taj Mahockey and Puckingham Palace.

The stuff that dreams are made of: Maple Leaf Gardens.

A FOND FAREWELL

February 13, 1999

Toronto ended its 68-year residence in Maple Leaf Gardens with a tender moment, as on this evening, Red Horner, who played in the first game at the Gardens in 1931 and was a key member of Toronto's first Stanley Cup victory that same season, offered a Maple Leaf banner to Leaf captain Mats Sundin. "Mats, take this flag to our new home," Horner said, "but always remember us."

Goodnight, Foster! Goalie Curtis Joseph looks out over ice once graced by King Clancy, Ace Bailey, Charlie Conacher, Teeder Kennedy, Syl Apps, Bill Barilko, Johnny Bower, Tim Horton, Dave Keon, Darryl Sittler, Lanny McDonald, Wendel Clark, Doug Gilmour and Mats Sundin.

We first heard about Wayne Gretzky during an *HNIC* item on the then-peewee star in 1971. (At 10, Wayne scored 320 goals in 69 games.) Next, he was star of Peter Gzowski's book *The Game of Our Lives*. Then, captain of the great Edmonton teams of the '80s, not to mention hero of international hockey wars. Finally, there were stops in Los Angeles, St. Louis and New York. So it was inevitable that Gretzky's goodbye weekend felt like a national retirement party. On Saturday night, Ron MacLean wandered into a hockey crowd in Montreal to talk to Rocket Richard and Jean Beliveau about Wayne, only to have Boom Boom Geoffrion grab the mike to extend personal regards to Wayne and Janet Gretzky. Then, the next day in New York, where number 99 played his last game, Bryan Adams offered up "O Canada" as a gentle, affecting lullaby. Appropriately, the pre-game ceremony was full of big, sloppy embraces. And it was wonderful seeing representatives of Gretzky's Edmonton dynasty — Mark Messier and Glen Sather — giving Wayne affectionate bear hugs.

Gretzky managed to collect a point this game, as you knew he would, setting up a score with a lovely, no-look pass. As the final seconds wound down on Wayne's on-ice career, the Madison Square Garden crowd stood up and gave the hockey hero a prolonged ovation, capping what was an entirely satisfying, weekend-long going-away party. In every interview, Wayne looked happy with his decision. As George Vescey wrote in a *New York Times* column, "In life as in hockey, Wayne Gretzky could see the entire rink. It was time to retire while he was still the Great One."

Above: Wayne Gretzky pulls away from long-time Islander nemesis, Denis Potvin. Below: A final salute from the greatest hockey player of all time.

Brett Hull (22) skates into the crease after a Dominek Hasek rebound to score the Cup-winning goal. The game would be over soon, but the arguments continue to this day.

It was a great game and better overtime. The Buffalo Sabres, led by bend-in-any-direction goalie Dominik Hasek, and the glittering Dallas Stars remained stuck in a one-all triple-overtime tie, game six of the Stanley Cup finals.

Then catastrophe. A goal-mouth scramble. Hasek down. Brett Hull gets a stick on the puck. It's in. Game and Stanley Cup over! But what's this? A replay review showed Hull's skate was over the line when the puck went in. This was a circumstance that at the time led to freeze-frame replays while review judges engaged in Socratic debate on what came first — the goal or the skate?

But this time there was no review and no debate, not at first anyway. And the goal counted. What happened?

According to HNIC executive director John Shannon, the NHL and broadcast simply got swept away by the tide of victory.

"Remember in a decisive Cup game, you're talking about the Normandy invasion once that goal is scored," he says. "We immediately sent 10 people onto the ice, and more into the winning dressing room. Once the Zamboni entrance is opened, the floodgates open. Everybody races to do their job. ... You're consumed by what happens next, not what happened two minutes ago."

Adds Ron MacLean, "There was such a crush to the ice, I remember feeling that if I didn't get there first, I wasn't going to get there at all."

A few minutes later, Shannon received a dispiriting message from reporter Scott Oake. The Sabres had watched the replay and wanted a review.

At 1:30 in the morning, EST, Harry Neale went on air and concluded the goal shouldn't have counted. But by then most viewers had drifted off in search of pillows. For Sabres fans, however, the controversy would never be put to bed.

He'd come back before, from a broken wrist, a chronic bad back, even cancer, but now, three-and-a-half-year years after retiring, Mario Lemieux had to fight time and the sure erosion of physical skills in returning to the NHL. Some felt the comeback was folly. No one could announce they were returning after that long a layoff, midway in the season, with a scant three weeks' preparation. No one except Mario, it turns out. First game back, against Toronto, he set up a goal 33 seconds into the contest, then later one-timed a neat back pass from Jaromir Jagr, finding the short side against Leaf goalie Curtis Joseph. Number 66 collected three points this evening, living up to his nickname, "Mario the Magnificent," one more time.

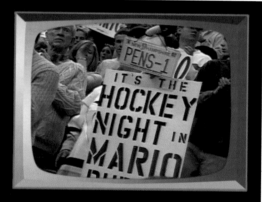

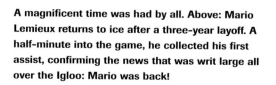

A magnificent time was had by all. Above: Mario Lemieux returns to ice after a three-year layoff. A half-minute into the game, he collected his first assist, confirming the news that was writ large all over the Igloo: Mario was back!

RAY DAY
June 9, 2001

A public institution in Boston, Ray Bourque was selected a first or second all-star his first 18 seasons, an NHL record. The five-time winner of the Norris Trophy also ended his career as Boston's point and assist leader. But never in his 21 seasons with the Bruins did he win a Stanley Cup — a situation that prompted him to agree to a trade to Colorado late in the 1999–2000 season. He didn't win the Cup that year, but the following season the 40-year-old defenceman played a crucial role in Colorado's come-from-behind, seven-game win over New Jersey. After accepting the Stanley Cup, Avalanche captain Joe Sakic then handed the trophy to Bourque, who burst into tears upon finally throwing the trophy over his head in triumph.

Montreal-born Ray Bourque and former Habs great, Patrick Roy, hoist the Stanley Cup in Rocky Mountain Time.

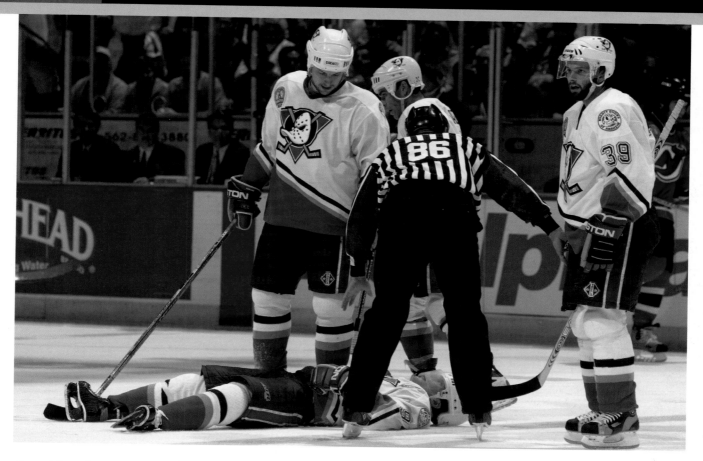

Considered too small for junior hockey, Paul Kariya won the **Paul Kariya is down, but not out.** Hobey Baker Award for outstanding play in U.S. college hockey before becoming the Mightiest Duck in Anaheim. After helping Canada to a gold medal in 2002, he provided the most memorable moment in the 2003 Stanley Cup finals. Intercepting a pass at centre in game six, Kariya sped off, passing to a teammate as he approached the Devils' blueline. He was following that pass when Scott Stevens, the NHL's most accomplished thumper, appeared, sliding onto our screens with his shoulder high. *Fmmp!* A half-minute later, Kariya twitched awake as if surfacing from deep sleep. Still, as teammates carried him off, the forward's legs were like dangling strands of spaghetti. He's not coming back, we figured. But before the period was over, there came a great stirring and Bob Cole shouted with evident surprise, "Paul Kariya is back!" Then, the little forward found a loose puck and open room up the left boards. Once inside the blueline, he wound up and fired a sure, hard slapshot high over Martin Brodeur's outstretched glove. Even a Duck Pond crowd weaned on fictitious kid-movie heroics was overwhelmed by the bravery and skill Paul Kariya displayed in coming back from the cooling board to score a big Stanley Cup goal.

GRADUATION SPEECH

February 21, 2002

Maybe the best TV moment at the 2002 Olympics came after the women's gold medal game, a match that saw Team Canada upset an American team that had beaten them eight straight by a score of 31–13. Huddled with her flushed, triumphant players, coach Danièle Sauvageau offered a stirring graduation speech: "You're going to go through tough times in life. Come back with responsibility, determination and courage. And don't ever, *ever* give up on [yourself]."

Canadian Olympic team coach Danièle Sauvageau is surrounded by her celebrating charges moments after Canada's 3–2 gold medal win over the United States. Below: Jayna Hefford scores on U.S. netminder Sara DeCosta, with a second left in the second period.

HOCKEY AFTERNOON IN UTAH February 24, 2002

Don Cherry and Ron MacLean were in Ron's hotel room the night before the 2002 Canada-U.S men's gold medal hockey game going through lineups and a six-pack of beer, when MacLean, normally the partner least given to proclamations, announced, "I don't think we can lose. Unless Richter ... "

"We're going to smoke 'em!" Cherry boomed.

The combatants of *Coach's Corner* are friends. The beer and banter are a road ritual.

Winning smiles: the Canadian men's team show the flag and bask in the glow of their gold medal moment.

Which is why, the next day on air, minutes before the gold medal game, and just after Cherry told us Canada "was gonna smoke 'em!" MacLean had a question left. "What's the final score?"

"Geez, you trying to get me in trouble?"

No, just out on a limb. "People enjoy Don's snap opinions," MacLean explains.

Cherry figured Canada would win by "a couple." MacLean felt Canada would win decisively on the strength of a pre-game expedition. "I showed up at 11 a.m. — two hours before game time — and there was no one in the rink," he says. "It was surreal. But with the Olympics, everyone was using an international feed. And CBC didn't have a lot of packages prepared because ... well, who knew we'd be playing for gold?"

Minutes later, MacLean saw his first omen: the second visitor to the rink was Wayne Gretzky.

"Team Canada wasn't prepared for how fast Olympic games unfolded in 1998 at Nagano," MacLean says. "Without commercials and short intermissions, the game is over in a heartbeat." Which is why he found it comforting to see Team Canada's GM there so early. Ready.

"We're gonna win," MacLean told Gretzky.

Joe Sakic snaps a shot past Mike Richter to give Canada a late 5–2 lead. "Surely, that's gotta be it!" cried *HNIC*'s Bob Cole in announcing the goal. It was.

"Know what'd be great?" Wayne responded. "If we win by a couple, so Canada savours the win."

MacLean didn't have to wait long to see if Canadian players were as confident as their GM. "I was standing against the glass when the players came out and one of the first to fly by, Owen Nolan, gave me a wink," he recalls.

Although Canada dominated early, U.S. scored first, with Canada tying it on a goal that will be replayed forever. It happened so fast that a week later HNIC was still taking calls from radio stations wanting to know if Mario Lemieux had indeed pretended to accept a sharp pass from Chris Pronger to lure out goalie Mike Richter, then allowed the puck through his skates to wide-open Paul Kariya for the score.

"I admit I didn't see it," MacLean says. "Don did. So did Bob Cole. I could hear him on my earpiece. But that's Bob. He can anticipate a play like a great player."

Canada controlled play, but enjoyed only a 3–2 lead, late. When asked why he kept reminding us of the slender lead through the third period, Cole chuckles. "You never let the audience off the hook," he says. "You've got to know when to tighten the screws."

And when to loosen them, and let an audience "savour the win," in Gretzky's words. This is how Cole, who had been taught by Foster Hewitt in the fifties to save his most passionate delivery for the game's climax, called the final goal: "Joe Sakic COMING RIGHT IN. SCORES! JOE SAAKICCC scores. And that makes it 5–2, Canada. Surely that's gotta be it."

Cole quieted down and allowed the Canadian portion of the Utah crowd's singing of "O Canada" to fill the last minute. Afterward, he turned to partner Harry Neale with a deadpan query that ushered us into the easy-feeling, national celebration that followed.

"So Harry, glad you came?"

Cherry and MacLean were. In fact, they enjoyed the game so much they watched it again that night on TV in Ron's room. "Ordinarily, Don is very disciplined — three beers each, and lite beers at that, is all we're allowed," he says. "That night I had a few more."

Doubleheaders Come to *Hockey Night in Canada*

For the 1994/95 season, *Hockey Night in Canada* launched a new doubleheader format (two games back to back) showing Eastern games followed by Western games. This set-up added greater exposure to the Canadian teams for the devoted fans across the country. CBC controlled everything from a mobile unit, and the commentators were on-site to experience the games. The country was connected by satellite, and viewers watched people carrying on conversations with each other from places as far away as Vancouver and Montreal — it was magic. Legends were made as stories were told through isolation and through pictures, by people right at the games.

A day and night in the life

Every Saturday night for the past 51 years, from the fall to late spring, fans from coast-to-coast-to coast have gathered in front of their television sets for a weekly ritual — CBC's HOCKEY NIGHT IN CANADA. What the viewers don't see is the hard work that begins, for dozens of technicians, producers, directors and of course the talent, long before the games begin and ends long after the final siren has gone off.

9 a.m. ET – The 52-foot long CBC Sports mobile arrives for a game at the Air Canada Centre and stations itself in the bowels of the arena. Another mobile arrives at the site of Game Two of the doubleheader — usually Calgary, Edmonton or Vancouver. The mobile truck resembles a NASA control room complete with dozens of monitors, videotape machines and enough high tech software to make Bill Gates jealous.

Technicians begin setting up the cameras, ensure all the tape machines and monitors are working correctly, and set up the lighting in the HNIC studio, located between the Maple Leafs' and visiting team's dressing rooms.

10:30 a.m. ET – Producers, directors and commentators attend the morning skate to look for possible line combinations, scratches from the lineup and, after the skate, for casual discussions with coaches and players to gather valuable information for the broadcast. The process is repeated by the Western crew prior to their game.

1 p.m. ET – Production begins in the mobile—voicing the features, such as *The Headliner*, and packaging items graphics that will appear in the pre-game show and the games.

2 p.m. ET – Ron MacLean arrives at the ACC and heads to the studio where he goes over updated NHL stats, talks with the producer about the lineup for the pre-game show, *Saturday Night*, and gathers his thoughts for the upcoming *Satellite Hot Stove* taping.

2:30 p.m. ET – Taping begins for the *Satellite Hot Stove* that airs in the second period of Game One.

5 p.m. ET – Don Cherry arrives at the ACC and goes over his pre-taped segments for his *Coach's Corner* segment in the HNIC studio.

5:30 p.m. ET – Rehearsal begins for the opening of the pre-game show.

6:30 p.m. ET – The CBC Sports opening montage hits the airwaves, and MacLean voices the intro to *Saturday Night*. In the mobile, producers and the director call out the camera angles they want for the next shot and the videotape operators ready the packaged items (e.g. *The Headliner*) for airing. Viewers also hear from Scott Oake and Kelly Hrudey who provide an early sense of things to come from Game Two.

7 p.m. ET – MacLean throws to Bob Cole and Harry Neale, who arrive at the rink at around 5:30 p.m., to provide the commentary from high above the ACC.

7:40 p.m. ET – MacLean and Cherry get prepared for the weekly *Coach's Corner* segment.

8:30 p.m. ET – The pre-taped *Satellite Hot Stove* segment airs.

9:30 p.m. ET — Game One of the doubleheader concludes and interaction between Game One and Game two begins. Viewers get post game reaction and interviews from Game One and we also check in on the pre-game skate at Game Two with Chris Cuthbert and Greg Millen and preview the matchup with Scott Oake and Kelly Hrudey.

10:00 P.M. ET — MacLean hands over the show to the Western crew. Oake and Hrudey lead things off with a "scene set" and Cuthbert and Millen call the action.

10:30 p.m. ET — MacLean and the Game One crew record *Scoreboard Saturday*, to air in the second intermission of Game Two.

11 p.m. ET — Following a long day, the crew from Game One start shutting down the equipment, leaving the "Western team" to close out the production of their game. This includes Hrudey's *Behind the Mask* segment and following the game the interactive post-game show, *After Hours*.

1:30 a.m. ET — The games are over and the Western crew brings the production to a close.

So, the next time you're sitting in front of your television set watching CBC's *Hockey Night in Canada*, you may not have the "best seat in the house." It may just belong to one of the talented and hardworking crew-members who began his or her day more than 14 hours ago.

CBCsports

NORTHERN NIGHTS

Ken Danby had the enthusiasm for a *Hockey Night in Canada* image long before CBC executives approached him, in 2001, about a painting to commemorate their fiftieth anniversary. "Years ago, I sketched an idea for a painting of individuals excitedly watching a *Hockey Night in Canada* broadcast. The concept remained in my mind, but as time passed it was left unresolved," Danby once explained.

"This painting is not intended to depict a particular time period, but to represent the entire era of 50 years of *HNIC*," the artist comments. "That it's a painting of Paul Henderson's series-winning goal in Moscow doesn't necessarily mean that the children are watching the live broadcast, as it has been shown numerous times since.

"The background offers a night sky filled with stars, symbolic of the hockey heroes and luminaries who have entertained us over the years. Canada's northern lights flare up from the horizon and accentuate the figure of a unique constellation in the shape of a hockey player raising the Stanley Cup high above his head—the ultimate goal of every player—sharing his celebration with all fans of the game."

Ken Danby Studios and the CBC jointly created reproduction prints to benefit minor hockey in Canada. The first prints were presented in 2002 to the newest inductees into the Hockey Hall of Fame.

HOCKEY DAY IN CANADA

In 1999, *HNIC* began taking time every season to travel from big league arenas to small town rinks and communities across the country. In 2002, "Hockey Day in Canada" examined the state of the game in Iqaluit, Nunavut. The accompanying photos show *Coach's Corner* sparring partners Don Cherry and Ron MacLean holding a hockey clinic in a community centre (top, left). The always-formal Cherry also took time to give the thumbs up to a local kids' team (top, right).

As part of Hockey Day, kids were asked to send in their drawings of what *Hockey Night in Canada* meant to them. The response was overwhelming. These are two of the entries. Left: Terra Failick, age 10. Right: Emily Hudson, age 13.

PHOTO CREDITS

INDEX